To April, for giving me love and encouragement and adding meaning to my life. You are pure joy and I can't imagine life without you.

To Summer, Brooke, Lily, and Grace, your mom and I have loved you since we first laid eyes on you, and we always will. You fill us with pride.

To my mom, Elaine, for your complete and total support. To my dad, Jack (1934–2016), for being the kind of father I could always look up to. And to my sister, Diane, for always being there.

"John Delaney's book is a practical and optimistic look at the future of our country, and how he sees us moving forward with solutions, not divisions. I always say we should be building bridges, not walls, and he is working every day to put that into practice. Delaney is an inspiration to us all—he is a true leader in a world that needs more leadership."

—**José Andrés**, chef/owner, ThinkFoodGroup and minibar by José Andrés, and founder, World Central Kitchen

"In these times of severe and destructive partisanship the American people have a unique opportunity to be represented by a man who represents the best of what has truly made us great: a desire to work together for solutions, a proven belief in free enterprise, hard work and commonsense all coupled with compassion. John Delaney's book is a starting point for the possibilities of this unlikely candidate."

—former representative **Richard L. Hanna** (R-New York)

"John Delaney has been a leader in finding innovative, bipartisan solutions to both help real people live better lives and to measure outcomes, so we know what works and what doesn't. This book provides a road map to refocus government to deliver on a more promising future rather than accepting the divided and dysfunctional status quo."

—**Sonal Shah**, executive director, Beeck Center for Social Impact and Innovation, Georgetown University, and former director of the White House Office of Social Innovation and Civic Participation

"John Delaney is a rare breed of politician who understands that we get the best outcomes for our citizens when the government, the private sector, and the nonprofit world work together. This book shows how his understanding of all three spheres makes him a leader who can make progress against the challenges we face."

—**Jim Sorenson**, founder and CEO, Sorenson Impact Foundation

The Right Answer

The Right Answer

How We Can Unify
Our Divided Nation

John K. Delaney

HENRY HOLT AND COMPANY   NEW YORK

Henry Holt and Company, LLC
Publishers since 1866
175 Fifth Avenue
New York, New York 10010
www.henryholt.com

Henry Holt® and 🔲® are registered trademarks of
Macmillan Publishing Group, LLC.

Library of Congress Cataloging-in-Publication Data is available.

ISBN: 978-1-25029-496-8

Our books may be purchased in bulk for promotional, educational, or business
use. Please contact your local bookseller or the Macmillan Corporate and Premium
Sales Department at (800) 221-7945, extension 5442, or by e-mail at
MacmillanSpecialMarkets@macmillan.com.

First Edition 2018

Designed by Kelly S. Too

Printed in the United States of America

1 3 5 7 9 10 8 6 4 2

CONTENTS

Prologue: The Courage of Our Convictions   1

1: Tell the Truth   7

2: Embrace Compromise   23

3: Open the Door   47

4: Harness the Power of Incentives   68

5: Think Different   89

6: Release America's Inner Entrepreneur   106

7: See Both Sides   127

8: Get Back to Governing   145

9: Focus on the Future   164

Epilogue: The Right Answer   196

Acknowledgments   209

Index   215

Let us not despair but act. Let us not seek the Republican answer or the Democratic answer but the right answer. Let us not seek to fix the blame for the past—let us accept our own responsibility for the future.

John F. Kennedy
Loyola College, Baltimore, Maryland
February 1958

The Right Answer

The Courage of Our Convictions

WEDNESDAY, AUGUST 1, 1923, DAWNED CHILLY AND CLEAR IN New York City. By the time the sun rose over lower Manhattan, a dozen passenger ships had steamed into New York Harbor, hurrying to complete the last leg of their long journeys across the Atlantic. And by the time the sun set, a total of sixteen such ships would dock at the city's piers, delivering fifteen thousand men, women, and children who dreamed of a better life in the United States of America.

These ships had sailed from all across Europe, and the people they carried came from every nation you could think of—Albania, Armenia, Britain, Egypt, Finland, Italy, Persia, Russia, Syria. As the *New York Times* put it the next day, "There were more than thirty-five nationalities represented by the immigrants who landed yesterday, and some of them spoke such strange tongues that no one so far has been found who can understand them."

The massive RMS *Franconia*, which had set out from Liverpool on July 22, carried the most passengers. Among its 3,200 travelers were a few minor celebrities, including the president of the Campbell Soup Company and a British tennis star. Also aboard the *Franconia* were eight members of the Rowe family of Quarrington Hill, England: thirty-six-year-old Emily Rowe and seven of her children, ranging in age from one-year-old Percival to seventeen-year-old Albert, known as Al. They were coming to meet Emily's husband, William, who'd arrived earlier and hoped to settle his family in New Jersey.

After ten days at sea, the Rowes had finally made it to Ellis Island, the first stop in their quest to become Americans. The family joined the crowds of people shuffling into the main building, up the staircase, and into the Great Hall, where doctors performed "six-second physicals," quick assessments to determine whether would-be immigrants were healthy enough to be allowed into the country. One by one, each of the Rowe children passed inspection, but when it was Al's turn the doctor stopped him. Al was missing his left arm, the result of a childhood accident, and that was enough for the authorities to order him detained.

Would Al be allowed to stay here with his family? Or would he be deemed unfit and sent back? It must have been frightening for this teenaged boy to know he could be put right back on a ship, alone, for the arduous return journey to England. He and his family had risked everything in the hope of making a new life in America. Now that it was almost within his grasp, was he destined to lose it?

At the family's request, Al was eventually granted an appeal, which would take place in Ellis Island's second-floor Hearing Room.

Taking a seat on a wooden bench, he watched nervously as the official who would decide his fate walked into the room. When he did, young Albert noticed something that stunned him. He could hardly believe his eyes, but the man hearing his case had only one arm.

And that was the moment when Al Rowe, my grandfather, knew he would be an American.

I LOVE THAT STORY ABOUT MY GRANDFATHER BECAUSE IT reminds me of just how hard generations of immigrants have fought to come to this country. The United States of America has always been a place worth striving toward, a place where people from all over the globe come to seek opportunity and build their futures.

It's a place where a young man such as Al Rowe could find a job and raise a family. Al worked at the Joseph Dixon Crucible Company, a pencil factory in Jersey City, New Jersey, for fifty years, supporting his family and passing along the values of hard work, honesty, and civility to his two children: my mother, Elaine, and my uncle John. It's a place where Elaine and her hardworking electrician husband, my father, Jack Delaney, could buy a home and raise their own children, including a son who would go on to become a lawyer, an entrepreneur, a CEO, a U.S. congressman, and now a candidate for president.

For two hundred fifty years, anything has seemed possible in the United States. Yet today our nation is deeply divided. More so than at any time in recent memory, our nation appears to be at war with itself. We're having a difficult time doing what we've always done best—respond to change, and lead.

The hard truth is that we're living in an era of hyperpartisan politics, and it's destroying our country. Particularly since the 2016 election, this rabid partisanship has been pulling communities apart; it's even pulling families apart. Worse, it's preventing us from seizing the large-scale opportunities that await the next generation, and it's making it impossible for us to address the urgent problems that are threatening our quality of life. Instead of rebuilding our country, we're tearing each other down. Instead of figuring out how to close the vast gap between rich and poor, we're busy figuring out how to blame the other side for our problems. Instead of developing global economic and security alliances, we're isolating ourselves from the rest of the world. Instead of preparing our citizens for the future of work, we're risking reduced economic growth with fewer paying jobs. And instead of adapting to new technological innovations, automation, and artificial intelligence, we're relitigating the decisions made in the past. Instead of leadership, we have divisiveness.

The cost of doing nothing is not nothing. The longer we delay addressing these problems, the worse they become. The longer we delay leading our country into the future, the more opportunities slip away. We have serious work to do, and our government is too focused on political gamesmanship to do it. Politicians these days seem to care more about the fight than about solutions, because fighting is what wins elections.

But the enemy is *not* the person on the other side of the aisle. The enemy is actually partisan politics itself. The American people are tired of it, and they are more than ready for change. In an October 2017 Gallup poll, a majority of respondents (58 percent) said they'd prefer their political leaders to "compromise in order to get things done," while just 18 percent said they'd prefer their leaders to "stick to their beliefs even if little gets done."

Clearly, the people are way ahead of the politicians on this issue. I've been in politics for only a few years, but I'm convinced that all this partisan fighting is based on the deeply flawed notion that the other side is always wrong. Even though I'm a strong Democrat, I don't think the Republicans are wrong about everything they believe. Succumbing to knee-jerk politics is the easy way out; instead, I believe we should look clearly at the facts and then identify solutions based on what's actually happening rather than on what might score political points.

I'm also an entrepreneur, so I tend to focus on the pragmatic question of how to get things done—and the way our government tries to get things done is, frankly, baffling to me. Imagine that you're trying to do business with someone and the first words out of your mouth are "You're stupid and everything you think is wrong. Now let's work out a deal." That would never fly in the business world, and it obviously doesn't work so well in politics, either. Why would you want to alienate the people you're trying to work with? Why not search for common ground, rather than harping on disagreements?

In other words, why not embrace bipartisanship and the truth? We've got to stop retreating to our corners and complaining about each other. At a crucial moment in our nation's history, we're looking for arguments when we need to be looking for solutions.

AFTER ALL THE POLITICAL FIGHTING, MUDSLINGING, AND pure hostility of the last few years, the central question is this: how can we bring the country back together again and start solving real problems to help real people? That's my goal as a candidate for the presidency, and that's what this book is about.

In these pages, I'll reveal nine ways we can work to unify our fractured nation. I'll describe big ideas and my proposed solutions for the most pressing problems facing us today. And I'll explain why I think I'm the person who can lead us where we need to go.

I've worn many hats in my professional life, first as a kid from a blue-collar family working summers on construction sites; then as a successful entrepreneur who founded and led companies that created thousands of jobs and brought in billions in revenue; then as a philanthropist; and then as a proud three-term U.S. congressman. I've spent my thirty-year career assessing tough problems, pivoting to innovative solutions, and leading with determination and optimism, and I want to bring that blend of experience to focus on the challenges facing America today.

I believe it's time for us to change direction. It's time to focus on the facts and on the future. It's time to discover the ideas we can agree on rather than hold tight to the beliefs that divide us. The truth is we agree on a lot more than we think we do. All of us want the same basic things, the very same things that brought a teenaged Al Rowe to these shores: a chance to make a living with dignity, to raise a family, and to embrace the unique opportunity that the United States of America has always offered. So let's figure out how to protect and strengthen those American ideals—together. Let's work together toward a common goal for the common good. Let's reject despair and choose action. That, as President Kennedy so memorably put it, is not the Democratic answer or the Republican answer, but the right answer for Americans today.

CHAPTER 1

Tell the Truth

The life of a nation is secure only while the nation is
honest, truthful, and virtuous.

FREDERICK DOUGLASS

IN THE WEEKS FOLLOWING PRESIDENT TRUMP'S INAUGURA-
tion in January 2017, many of us felt like America was being
torn in half. In response to the new president's divisive policies
and hurtful rhetoric, protest marches and demonstrations broke
out, pundits screamed at one another on TV, and the "Resist"
movement began gathering steam. People across the country
demanded town hall–style meetings so they could tell their elected
officials exactly where they thought our nation was headed. Some
politicians agreed to face their constituents, but many refused,
deciding it would be best to wait out the furor.

That February, I was scheduled to speak at an event for senior
citizens in Gaithersburg, Maryland. The previous fall, I had been

reelected by a comfortable margin, and now I was starting my third term as the U.S. representative for Maryland's Sixth District. The event, which we'd scheduled months ago, was a workshop where seniors could get practical help and advice on topics such as Social Security and Medicare eligibility and programs. We hadn't planned it as a town hall event, but because of the way things were going it had the potential to turn into one.

We were expecting about three hundred attendees and, given the topic and the particular location, I knew the audience would lean very liberal. I planned to open the workshop by telling the crowd about a bipartisan bill I was cosponsoring, which would set up a bipartisan commission aimed at extending the fiscal health of Social Security for seventy-five years, an issue that's very important to me. The bill follows a model employed by Ronald Reagan and Tip O'Neill in the early 1980s, when they successfully extended the fiscal health of Social Security for fifty years; since the passage of their bill, the poverty rate of seniors has been cut in half.

While my policy instincts are often considered progressive, my political instincts have always been bipartisan. I believe that my job as a member of Congress is to find the best ideas no matter where they reside, whether on the progressive or the conservative side or somewhere in between. I also strongly believe that legislation brought forth in a bipartisan way, with sponsors from both sides, has a better chance of succeeding in the short term and enduring in the long term.

During my second term, in fact, the independent site GovTrack.us ranked me as one of the most bipartisan members of Congress, a designation I was proud of. Under normal circumstances, I'd be happy to tell any audience that fact, but these weren't normal circumstances. Progressives were understandably furious with President Trump, and they certainly didn't seem to be in the mood for working together.

Just before the event began, I turned to a member of my team. "Do you think it would be a mistake to talk about bipartisanship right now?" I asked.

"Yeah," he replied. "Probably best not to bring it up. This group wants you to be a partisan."

Yet, as I stepped to the podium, that didn't feel right. Yes, Donald Trump had been elected president, but that wasn't going to stop me from working with the other side to get things done, so why should I pretend otherwise? Wasn't it better to tell the truth, no matter the consequences?

I started my speech by talking about my bipartisan work on Social Security. Then I went straight to it, saying, "I was rated the third most bipartisan member of the Congress last year, by the way, by an independent group."

I had no idea how the crowd would react to this news, but I didn't expect what happened next: the entire audience erupted into applause. Apparently, this was exactly what this liberal group wanted to hear—and it was a great reminder that telling the truth about where you stand is always the best option.

My father, Jack Delaney, died in the summer of 2016, but if you had met him you would have understood immediately why I tend to prefer straight talk.

Dad was born in Jersey City, New Jersey, the son of a dockworker and a bighearted mother. He was proud of his Irish heritage, and he grew up scrapping and playing sports, eventually

becoming a star high school football player in the town of Hasbrouck Heights. His high school sweetheart was a girl named
Elaine, a pretty student at the rival high school who'd been named
Miss Wood-Ridge of 1953. Elaine, too, was of Irish heritage, on
her mother's side, but her father, Al Rowe, was from England.

My parents married just after graduating high school in 1957.
Rather than going to college, they went right to work. Dad joined
the International Brotherhood of Electrical Workers as an electrician, a profession that provided him with a good living for sixty
years. My mother was a bank teller at Wood-Ridge National Bank
for a couple of years before giving birth to her first child, my sister,
Diane. Four years later, in 1963, I was born, and the four of us
lived in a Sears Roebuck house, the kind that people used to buy
out of the Sears catalogue and have assembled on their little plots
of land.

My father was a no-nonsense kind of guy—he had a strong
handshake, liked his sports, enjoyed having a beer with his buddies. Every day, he'd get up before dawn, put on his usual uni-
form of work boots, jeans, and a T-shirt or flannel shirt, and then
head out in his pickup truck to his current job site. Dad worked
hard at his trade, and he taught my sister and me that same work
ethic. He was also very good at his job: he became the foreman
on some of the biggest projects in northern New Jersey, including overseeing much of the electrical work in the old Giants
Stadium when it was constructed in the mid-1970s.

One of my favorite things to do as a boy was to go to work
with him, riding in his pickup truck with the big toolbox in the
back. He'd show me around the sites, teaching me the rudiments
of the electrician's trade and giving me small jobs to do. He showed
my sister, Diane, and me the value of hard work. In fact, I can't

remember a time as a kid when I wasn't working during breaks from school. I spent summers as a mason and excavation laborer, a painter, a landscaper, and most often as an electrician's assistant, working side by side with my father.

Dad was the strongest person I knew, always winning arm-wrestling competitions in local bars and performing feats of strength for his buddies. He wasn't a showboat, but he carried himself with pride and expected his fellow workers to treat him with respect. Usually they did. But one day, when I was about ten years old, I saw what happened when they didn't.

That morning, a Saturday, we hopped in the pickup truck and Dad drove us to a sprawling industrial job site. The project was well under way, and my dad's team had been running wires through the studs and installing hundreds of outlets. He wanted to check on their progress, but to his surprise he found carpenters installing Sheetrock on the walls.

My dad walked up to the foreman responsible for the carpenters. "What the hell is going on?" he asked. "You weren't supposed to do this for another two weeks. You've covered up all my outlets; I can't even find them." The foreman shrugged and said, "Too bad, Jack. The Sheetrock came in early, and I told my guys to put it up. Your problem, not mine."

At first, my dad just looked at him. Then he said, "Well, I guess I'll just have to find the outlets myself." Then I watched as he bent down, picked up a lump hammer, and smashed a hole into one of the walls. Then he smashed another, and another, each time saying, "Nope, no outlet here!" After he'd punched about a dozen holes in the freshly installed Sheetrock, the foreman took a swing at him, but Dad grabbed him by the shirt and knocked him to the ground with one punch. Just then, the project manager overseeing the whole job came running up. My dad turned to him, his eyes sparking with anger. "This is why you need union contractors," my dad said. "We work together."

My father worked hard and played hard, and he used to love going to the bar at the end of a long day on the job. He'd drink a few beers with his friends, an assortment of local electricians, plumbers, carpenters, and masons, and sometimes he stayed late enough that my mother would feel compelled to go get him. She'd bring me and my sister along, sending me into the bar to collect him as she sat outside in the car with the engine idling. I didn't mind; I knew all his buddies. I'd go in and say hello, and they'd all greet me with "Hey, Johnny!" And sometimes, if I was lucky, I'd get to hang out for a few minutes with my dad and his friends while he finished up.

Dad was also industrious. As a young electrician, he used to collect small pieces of discarded copper wire, which he'd take home in his lunch pail. Most of the pieces were two or three inches long, very heavy gauge (about a half inch to an inch thick) and covered with a heavy rubber outer jacket insulation. For months, he would stack them in a growing pile in our basement. When the pile got to be about four feet high, he'd spend hours after work skinning the rubber jackets off the scraps of wire with a pocket-knife. He'd stay up most of the night, and by the morning he'd have a pile of copper wire that we could sell by the pound. This was the early 1970s, when copper wire sold for about a dollar a pound, so we'd make several hundred dollars. The work was tedious and long, but I remember how proud I felt when he invited me to join him for this nighttime ritual.

My father's strong work ethic made it possible for him and my mom to save enough money to buy a second house, a two-family unit that later produced rental income. The place was completely dilapidated when they purchased it, and some of the happiest memories I have as a boy were of spending weekends together with my dad, fixing up that house.

While he didn't express it the same way most parents do today, my dad was a warm, caring, and loving father. Whenever Diane, my mom, or I was sick, he would always find a phone during the day so he could call to see how we were doing. After work, he'd bring us a present or a favorite food, and I can remember him cracking open the door to my room on many nights to check on me.

Much of who I am today I owe to my dad. He taught me to work hard, never to back down, to stand up for friends, and to care for and protect family. In his world, this was the code by which you judged yourself. And in everything he did, he was a straight shooter, a man who said what he meant and meant what he said, no matter the consequences.

ONE OF OUR GOVERNMENT'S BIGGEST PROBLEMS IS THAT IT makes decisions based not on facts, but on politics, emotions, and ideology. This leads to huge problems in governance because instead of creating smart policies we're creating partisan ones.

I've been an entrepreneur for three decades, and the experience of creating and building companies taught me a lot about the value of facts and the necessity of telling the truth. When starting a business, you have to be relentlessly honest. Is there a real opportunity? Do you have the resources to pursue it? Is your strategy working? You have to constantly analyze how you're doing, where you're succeeding, and where you're failing, and then adjust accordingly. If you try to fudge the answers to any of these questions, your venture will most likely fail; the more honest you are with yourself, the better your decision making will be.

I did my best to be objective—or, to put it another way, brutally honest—about the strengths and weaknesses of my businesses. Here's one example. In the summer of 2008, I was CEO of CapitalSource, a company with $4 billion in market value that I'd cofounded in 2000 and taken public three years later. Our business was providing loans to small and midsize companies, and over the eight years of the company's existence we'd had an amazing run. CapitalSource filled a real need in the market, and we'd helped finance thousands of companies, creating hundreds of thousands of jobs.

Then, in the late summer of 2008, the financial crisis struck. Confidence in the market began to plummet, and I knew our stock was going to take a massive hit. Some other financial companies tried to downplay or hide the extent of the potential damage in an effort to reassure their shareholders. I decided to go the opposite way.

Working with my team, I created a clear-eyed analysis of how our portfolio of loans was likely to perform based on the coming credit crisis and economic downturn, which we expected to be significant. We put our loans into categories, with detailed disclosures showing the balances, our reserves, and how much money we could expect to lose. We prepared aggressive estimates of just how bad the situation could get, and then we put it all out in the open for people to see. I believed that even though things were tough and about to get even more painful, CapitalSource would survive the crisis, provided we were honest. Though I hoped that this display of transparency would reassure our investors and bondholders that they could trust us, there was no way to know for sure.

We sent out our analysis via the required public disclosures, and while it caused anxiety in the short term, our honesty about the challenges we faced had the effect I'd hoped for. The fact that we'd communicated with our stakeholders with total transparency helped to restore confidence, and, thanks to this and other factors, our company ultimately rode out the financial crisis, one of the few financial services companies that was able to do so. We avoided any defaults, paid back all our debts, continued to grow our business, and didn't take any money from the government, even though we were eligible for it. By comparison, our main competitor, a company called CIT, ultimately had to file for bankruptcy, even after receiving a massive government bailout.

Telling the truth is a smart strategy in business, and in government. If we want to restore trust with the American people, we need to communicate directly and honestly with them.

TELLING THE TRUTH IS A TRAIT THAT SEEMS TO BE IN SHORT supply in American politics these days. Each party basically tells lies about the other, insisting that the other side is invariably corrupt, stupid, naive, or just wrong about everything. These messages have the short-term goal of winning elections, but they do lasting damage by eroding people's trust in their government.

The U.S. government is unique in the history of the world, and as such it has long been a source of great pride for Americans. Our Founding Fathers didn't invent democracy, but they did create a better version of it—one that, two hundred fifty years later, endures and remains the envy of the world. Our three equal branches of government, and the checks and balances they provide, have granted us unprecedented stability, security, and economic prosperity, and the Founders' intentional decentralization of power has kept us safe from autocracy. And while our system is not perfect, it does work, despite what we all hear to the contrary these days.

It's important to understand how much the U.S. government's evolution was influenced by two factors: the eight-year Revolutionary War that overthrew the British monarchy in favor of democracy and the never-ending battle between those who want to invest more power in the states and those who want to invest more in the federal government. These two factors led to the creation of a system of government that requires broad support, not merely a simple majority, before anything can get done. In other words, the success of our government requires broad buy-in—and right now, we don't have much of that.

In 1986, President Reagan gave voice to many people's mistrust of government when he said, "I've always felt the nine most terrifying words in the English language are 'I'm from the government, and I'm here to help.'" And it's not just conservatives who feel that way. According to Pew research, Americans' trust in the federal government is approaching an all-time low and keeps on dropping. These days, a majority of Americans sees our government as dysfunctional, corrupt, and unresponsive to their needs, when it should be accomplishing precisely the opposite: we should be engaging in the transformational work of bettering lives.

The American people have correctly diagnosed that we have a problem. But the remedy they've chosen, Donald Trump, is completely incapable of fixing it. If anything, the hyperpartisan, "alternative-facts" universe that the Trump presidency has ushered in has made things materially worse. And that has led to a national crisis of confidence. As Americans, we identify closely with our ideals and history. When we lose faith in our government, we also lose faith in ourselves.

So, what can we do to restore that faith? The first step is to tell the American people the truth. Here are just two ways I would do that within the first one hundred days of my presidency.

1. Engage in open, televised debates with members of Congress

If you've ever watched the Prime Minister's Question Time in the British Parliament, you will understand what I am proposing. Once a week, the prime minister appears in the Commons Chamber and, for thirty to forty-five minutes, takes whatever questions the members of Parliament and the House of Lords want to ask. There's nothing flashy about the process; the prime minister is down in the trenches, surrounded by shouting, hissing, applauding people. There's no hiding, no obfuscating. The give-and-take is chaotic but genuine. If the prime minister doesn't know the facts or the issues, it is painfully clear to everyone.

Compare this to our current system of White House press briefings. A few times a week, the president's press secretary stands in front of the White House press corps and, in theory, answers questions. In reality, these press briefings have devolved into propaganda sessions. The press secretary often deflects legitimate queries, and rarely do reporters have a chance to ask meaningful follow-up questions. For a while, the Trump administration banned television cameras from the briefing; they actually wanted to move the cameras out of the White House. The administration has also played favorites when choosing the reporters who get to ask questions. This isn't the kind of truth-telling session the American people deserve.

The American president also communicates with the nation through a weekly radio address, which, in the Internet age, has become a weekly YouTube or FaceTime Live video. But here's a question for you: When is the last time you watched one of those? Did you even know they still existed? These are three- to five-minute written speeches, with the president sitting and looking into the camera, and very few people pay attention to them. Who wants to spend time watching a canned weekly speech?

For those who prefer more spontaneous, off-the-cuff pronouncements, our current president obliges almost daily on Twitter. Unfortunately, there is often little truth in his tweets, and it's virtually impossible to break through the cacophony on Twitter and have any meaningful debate about what he's written. Instead, his tweets are debated vociferously on cable news shows, with the president nowhere in sight, safe from having to defend or back up whatever claims he's made.

What I'm proposing is something substantively different from all this. As president, I would engage once a quarter, for two to three hours, in a televised open debate with members of Congress. The American people deserve to hear real debate about real issues. They deserve to have a president who is unafraid to face the opposition, to hear other points of view, and to engage in constructive dialogue about how best to move forward. Transparency is the greatest tool for getting at the truth and bringing forth new ideas, so let's open the door to real debate and let the light shine in.

2. Deliver a true State of the Union address

Whenever I watch a president deliver a State of the Union address, I'm struck by the fact that no matter which party is in power, the speech usually has very little to do with the actual state of the union.

These annual addresses have become glorified campaign speeches, complete with planned applause lines and emotional acknowledgments of people planted in the audience. They're interrupted repeatedly by standing ovations, though usually from only one party. Think about it: these rare events bring together the men and women who serve at the highest levels of the executive, legislative, and judicial branches. Is conducting a partisan pep rally really the best use of everyone's time?

I believe the State of the Union address should be exactly what the title implies: a speech about what is truly happening in the nation. As president, I would describe the good *and* the bad, and offer prescriptions for how to fix what's broken. Instead of an exercise in patting the back of my administration, I'd offer a substantive policy agenda for further improving the state of the country. Let's save the campaigning for campaigns. We should take advantage of opportunities such as the State of the Union address to provide facts, introduce new ideas, and move the nation forward, rather than further divide it.

For example, if I were giving the State of the Union address today, I would start by talking about the crucial factors that are impeding our ability to prosper and lead. First up: our misdiagnosis of the issues associated with globalization and technological innovation.

Globalization has fundamentally changed our economy and

society over the past several decades. And although becoming more connected globally has been good for both the United States and humankind in general, it has also caused significant pain and suffering in large parts of our country and destabilized parts of the world. Acting as a great sorting machine, globalization has improved the world's standard of living, ushered in an era of innovation, driven tremendous economic growth in certain industries, and lifted billions of people out of poverty—but it has also disrupted communities and created great inequalities in economic opportunity. Because it has helped build a global middle class, it has contributed to keeping America safe. At the same time, though, the increasing ease of global connections has created new risks such as the ever more virulent spread of terrorism and epidemics.

The truth is politicians in both parties knew that while becoming part of a global economy would have numerous benefits, it would also cause hardship and pain for many people in our country. Democrats and Republicans alike failed to respond to the fears expressed by those who almost certainly would be hurt. We could have, and should have, handled this transition far better. In short, we didn't do our jobs.

There are two reasons why it's critical to address the challenges of globalization now. First, unless we honestly address the core issue—that is, how political gridlock has prevented us from responding to rapid change—we will undermine the benefits we've gained from a global system of institutions, alliances, and trade, benefits that have contributed enormously to American prosperity and security. Second, we are currently hurtling toward a similarly disruptive period, this time from technological innovation. As with globalization, Americans will enjoy many benefits from this new era, but if we fail to act, huge parts of our country will again be left behind.

As president, I would take active steps to deliver a long-overdue response to those hurt by globalization, while also focusing on how we can prevent something similar from happening again as the pace of technological change accelerates. We need a new social contract that will allow all Americans to feel more secure and to thrive in today's world.

I WANT TO MAKE A FINAL POINT ABOUT THE IMPORTANCE of telling the truth. Unfortunately, we find ourselves suffering through a period in American politics during which civility has gone out the window. The level of discourse has become less and less respectful, which diminishes our ability to work together and get things done. This trend is largely the result of decades of misrepresentations, with each side calling the other names and insisting not just that their ideas are wrong but that they are bad or even evil for suggesting them.

One of my fellow members of Congress is a medical doctor. A while ago, he left his surgical practice because he knew that after a certain age, he would find it difficult to maintain the hand-eye precision needed for surgery. After he stopped practicing medicine, he decided he'd like to do some good by serving the public, so he ran for Congress and won a seat.

This guy is a smart and accomplished person; he also happens to be a Republican who believes the Affordable Care Act is not working, something he and I completely disagree on. I think the Affordable Care Act, while imperfect and in need of improvement, has been a transformational step forward, one that significantly advances basic social justice. My colleague disagrees, so he's been working hard to try to repeal this legislation. As a result, he's taken a lot of heat from certain quarters. When speaking with him one afternoon, I was taken aback when he described to me the kinds of things people had said about him.

"They say I want to kill people," he told me, getting visibly upset. "I've spent my whole career saving people's lives, literally, in the operating room. It's what defines me." The slurs, he said, were hurtful and unfair. And he's right: we need to have open debates about policies, but we also need to draw the line and make it clear that calling someone a murderer because of his political beliefs is unacceptable.

A similar dynamic occurs whenever Democrats talk about gun safety. Even when we're proposing commonsense legislation, such as a law to keep guns away from people on the Terrorist Screening Center's no-fly list, gun proponents claim we're trying to take away everyone's guns. They never suggest that we simply have different views on how best to stop the ongoing carnage from gun violence in this country; instead, the other side pushes the rhetoric to an extreme level, claiming that we're trying to destroy the American way of life. It is not only absurd but also very damaging.

We have to stop lying about each other. When the level of discourse sinks this low, when our lack of civility leads to calling each other names, it damages our ability to work together. If we want our political system to work more smoothly, we have to restore honesty and civility. And that starts at the very top—with the president, who should represent every American.

CHAPTER 2

Embrace Compromise

Alone we can do so little; together we can do so much.

HELEN KELLER

Freshman members of Congress are a bit like freshmen in high school: low on the totem pole and, for the most part, expected to be seen and not heard. Yet, almost as soon as I took office in January 2013, I started working on a bill that had the potential to make waves. It was a big idea, focusing on two of the most divisive issues in American politics: taxes and spending policy. Even so, my goal was to get an equal number of Republican and Democrats to cosponsor it.

At first, the only thing people from both sides of the aisle could agree on was that I had zero chance of achieving my goal. Everyone I talked to, from fellow members of Congress to staff to lobbyists, thought I was aiming too high. When I described my plan to one longtime member of Congress, she actually laughed. This just wasn't how things worked. I knew that, but I also thought: They *should* work this way. So why not try?

At the time, Republicans controlled the House, Democrats controlled the Senate, and President Obama was in the White House. To me, it seemed that the only way to get anything done was to attract bipartisan support. My bill, which would improve our crumbling infrastructure through an innovative plan to repatriate cash that American companies were keeping overseas, had elements that could appeal to both sides. Figuring that the only way to get support was to go out there and earn it, I approached the challenge using the strategy that made the most sense to me, even if it was one that no one else in Congress seemed to be using.

First, I put together a PowerPoint presentation, preparing my pitch much the same way I would have done when I worked in the private sector. Then I asked for meetings with every Republican in the House—all 233 of them—so I could go to their offices, one by one, and pitch my bill. This was a time-consuming, repetitive task, but it was the only way I knew to persuade Republicans that the bill was worth supporting. Most meetings were planned, but occasionally I'd drop by someone's office to introduce myself, chat a little bit, and mention the bill. Over the next few months, I met with a total of about 150 Republican members, and one of the comments I heard over and over was "No one does this," usually followed by a remark of appreciation that I'd taken the time to come meet with them personally.

One of the first members I met with liked the bill, but no one else had signed on yet, and he couldn't get comfortable with the idea of taking the lead. Undeterred, we kept on trying. I truly believed if we could get that first Republican member to sign on, others would follow.

"Grinding out the details" is an expression I've always liked, and there's no doubt it has guided my business career. If you look at the two companies I cofounded and took public, neither of them was built around easy, obvious ideas that were bound to work. They were both lending companies focused on small to midsize businesses, and, as such, they had competition from other companies that'd been in the business longer. The only way we could succeed was to grind it out, by working harder and doing a better job than our competitors.

When I was growing up, my mother tried to drum this work ethic into my sister and me. She'd often say, "The dictionary is the only place where you'll find the word *success* before the word *work*." And my father put this principle into action very memorably one summer, when he built me a treehouse with no ladder— and in fact no tree. He built a small playhouse on poles, so the only way to get up to it was by climbing a rope. "If you can't get up there," he told me, "then you don't deserve to be up there." That set the pattern for me: if I wanted something badly enough, I had to work until I found a way to get it.

Dad also taught me that sometimes success comes through grinding it out. As much as I loved going to his job sites, and as much as I learned about the electrician's trade, some of the work he had me do was downright boring. But if an electrician's work is sometimes tedious, it's always necessary. You can't cut corners when wiring a house or a building.

One summer, Dad's employer got a contract to undertake some maintenance work at Fairleigh Dickinson University in New Jersey. I was able to get a job helping out, and he assigned me the task of painting the boiler room floors. But you can't just slap new paint over the old, so the first part of my job was scraping off all that old gray industrial paint. I was hunched over for hours, scraping and scraping in the heat, and at one point I had to crawl under one of the big boilers to scrape the floor there. I was tired, sweaty, and shirtless, and when I lost focus for just a second, I lifted myself up off my stomach just enough to touch the blazing hot boiler. For an awful moment, I was stuck to it, and the result was a blistering burn across my entire back. After getting bandaged up at the local medical clinic, I returned to the boiler room, scraping and painting until that floor was finished.

I took that same determination into my career as an entrepreneur, and as a new congressman I counted on it to help improve my chances for success with the infrastructure bill. I knew that if we could build bipartisan support and pass this bill, we could do a lot of good for the American people. Somehow, we had to get past the ingrained hyperpartisanship that was constantly obstructing our progress—and that George Washington himself warned us about more than two centuries ago.

IN THE FALL OF 1796, GEORGE WASHINGTON DECLINED TO be considered for a third term as president of the United States. He made his decision official in a letter that later became known as his Farewell Address. The letter was published in the newspaper *Claypoole's American Daily Advertiser* on September 19, and soon thereafter, Washington retired to his home in Mount Vernon.

Washington's Farewell Address is one of the most amazing essays I have ever read. It is remarkable in two ways. First is the fact that he wrote it at all: rather than running for a third term as president, he chose to withdraw from the political arena. Washington was hugely popular, and he could easily have continued to lead the country as an almost kinglike figure. The American people would have accepted this: they were used to a king; they understood a king. But Washington knew that his staying on indefinitely would be detrimental to our fledgling democracy, so he took it upon himself to stand down.

His Farewell Address is remarkable also for its prescient warning to Americans about the dangers of hyperpartisanship. Even in those early days of the nation, Washington could see that our shared purpose was being undercut by vicious partisan fighting. In the text, he goes straight to the heart of the matter, writing first about the dangers of lying while engaged in the political process.

> One of the expedients of party to acquire influence within particular districts is to misrepresent the opinions and aims of other districts. You cannot shield yourselves too much against the jealousies and heartburnings which spring from these misrepresentations; they tend to render alien to each other those who ought to be bound together by fraternal affection.

He also wrote about what he called the "baneful effects of the spirit of party generally." Washington knew that the existence of political parties was inevitable, "having its root in the strongest passions of the human mind." But he took pains to warn about the ways in which parties could undermine our democratic government.

> The alternate domination of one faction over another, sharpened by the spirit of revenge, natural to party dissension,

which in different ages and countries has perpetrated the most horrid enormities, is itself a frightful despotism. But this leads at length to a more formal and permanent despotism. The disorders and miseries which result gradually incline the minds of men to seek security and repose in the absolute power of an individual; and sooner or later the chief of some prevailing faction, more able or more fortunate than his competitors, turns this disposition to the purposes of his own elevation, on the ruins of public liberty.

A later paragraph is so apropos of our current political situation that it's difficult to believe Washington wrote it more than two hundred years ago.

[Partisanship] serves always to distract the public councils and enfeeble the public administration. It agitates the community with ill-founded jealousies and false alarms, kindles the animosity of one part against another, foments occasionally riot and insurrection. It opens the door to foreign influence and corruption, which finds a facilitated access to the government itself through the channels of party passions. Thus the policy and the will of one country are subjected to the policy and will of another.

Washington was not unaware of the value of political parties, as he makes clear elsewhere in his address. But the list of dangers he associates with hyperpartisanship is long, and while he never uses the word *bipartisanship*—it wasn't coined until the early twentieth century—he obviously advocates for those of opposing political views to work together. In fact, he warns in dramatic terms of the dangers of hyperpartisanship.

> [T]here being constant danger of excess, the effort ought to be by force of public opinion, to mitigate and assuage it. A fire not to be quenched, it demands a uniform vigilance to prevent its bursting into a flame, lest, instead of warming, it should consume.

"Bursting into a flame" seems an apt if unfortunate metaphor for our political situation today. We're so busy indulging in hyperpartisan fighting that we aren't coming together to solve our mutual problems. In effect, we're standing by and watching as our democracy threatens to go up in smoke.

To be clear, I'm a proud Democrat. I've chosen to be a Democrat because the party's values line up with my belief that we should strive for a more socially just society; maintain institutions that protect the poor, support workers, and improve our environment; protect the right of women to make their own health care and reproductive decisions; and support equality and civil rights in all forms. But my orientation is to work across the aisle to achieve these goals, rather than simply to fight the other side.

OF COURSE, IF YOU SERVE IN CONGRESS IT'S NOT ENOUGH just to talk to members of both parties and *hope* they can come together. In order to win bipartisan support for a bill, you have to offer something of value to both sides. You have to make sure each party can claim a "win." This conviction was at the forefront of my thinking as I crafted my infrastructure bill.

In 2012, when I was first running for my congressional seat, the country was still experiencing slow economic growth. I started to think seriously about what I could do to make a difference economically, and infrastructure seemed an obvious choice. Not only is it the biggest public investment our country makes, but it also has the second-highest return on investment of any government expenditure. (Research is the highest.) And I knew that over the past few decades, although our investment in infrastructure had gone up in absolute dollars, when expressed as a percentage of our economy it had actually, and shockingly, been cut by half.

You could see the ramifications of this neglect everywhere. Commute times were long because roads and bridges were in poor shape. Children in rural areas couldn't get broadband, and this hampered their chances to succeed in school. And though it hadn't become national news yet, people in Flint, Michigan, were getting poisoned because of their deteriorating water system, a situation that many poor urban kids confront on a daily basis. All across the country, citizens were suffering, even as our investment in fixing these problems was shrinking.

The failure to invest in infrastructure was also contributing to another serious problem. Then as now, our country was adding jobs at a rapid rate, but we still weren't creating enough middle-class jobs. If you broke down the numbers, most new jobs were either high-skill, high-pay work or low-skill, low-pay work. If you plotted it on a graph, you'd see a barbell shape that leaves out the middle class, which has long been the economic majority of our country and is central to overall American prosperity.

Infrastructure disproportionately creates middle-skill, middle-class jobs. Not surprisingly, many of these jobs are in industries such as construction, but they're also in manufacturing. Think about it: a lot of the parts and machinery we need for infrastructure, things such as sewer pipes and the large pieces of metal reinforcing bridges, are too big and heavy to transport profitably from other countries, so it's best to make them here in the United States. But if we're not investing in upgrading those sewers or fixing those bridges, those jobs never materialize.

Our world-class infrastructure was one of the most important drivers of our competitive economic strength throughout the twentieth century. It allowed our companies to grow, boosted their productivity, and, as a result, created higher living standards for our citizens. But the failure to maintain our infrastructure into the twenty-first century is crimping job creation and threatening our long-term competitiveness. Unless we improve America's infrastructure, we could lose even more investment and more jobs to other countries. In fact, while monetary policy has dominated global economics for the last several decades, I believe that infrastructure policy will dominate the next few. The country with the best portfolio of infrastructure assets, and the one that helps the developing world build theirs, will be best positioned to compete globally.

No one seriously disputes that we need to put more dollars into improving our infrastructure. But the question that accompanies this debate is always the same: How do we pay for it? In a government that's fiscally constrained, with high deficits and high debt, there's not a lot of appetite among Republicans to approve a spending program that increases the deficit just for this issue. They'll do it for taxes, using the classic (and deeply flawed) trickle-down argument that lowering taxes will grow the economy. The same argument could apply to increased investment in infrastructure, of course, but because it involves spending, Republicans typically don't want any part of it.

ONE THING MY BUSINESS CAREER TAUGHT ME IS THIS: WHEN you need money, go where the money is. As I was putting together my bill, I realized that a lot of the money was overseas.

For the first time in history, U.S. corporations were keeping more cash overseas than in the United States. By the end of 2013, domestic companies were parking approximately $2 trillion abroad; as of late 2017, that amount stood at almost $3 trillion, out of a total of about $4.5 trillion in cash. By the time you're reading this, that situation will most likely have changed, following the passage in late 2017 of the GOP tax bill. Later, I'll explain why that specific bill was flawed and a missed opportunity. For now, it's worth looking at how our broken international tax system caused all that cash to pile up overseas in the first place.

Let's say you were running a U.S.-based multinational company with operations both here and abroad. If you made $1 million here, you paid 35 percent tax, assuming you had no tax breaks. If you made $1 million in Germany, you paid the German corporate tax, which is 20 percent.

A company making $1 million in Germany and paying the 20 percent tax rate would net $800,000. Here's the problem. If the company then brought that money back to the United States, or "repatriated" it, it would have to pay the difference in the tax rates, which would mean ponying up an additional $150,000. But the U.S. tax code allowed companies to defer paying this tax if they elected not to repatriate the money. Companies didn't want to pay the additional tax, so they kept their money overseas.

Complicating this picture was the difference between companies that required physical locations abroad and those that didn't. Take Starbucks, for example, which operates coffee shops in Germany. If Starbucks paid 35 percent in corporate taxes while its German competitors were paying only 20 percent, it would be at a built-in disadvantage. Starbucks had to pay taxes in whichever country it was operating; if it was operating in a country with a lower corporate tax rate, it also had to pay the balance amount if it repatriated that money back to the United States, which creates a strong incentive to keep the profits abroad.

A company built around intellectual property, on the other hand, doesn't have to be tied down to any particular location. A powerful company such as Apple could approach various countries' governments and negotiate the best tax terms possible—and because even a small percentage of Apple's revenue would be a tremendous boon to just about any country, the offered terms were likely to be very favorable. Moreover, Apple had the upper hand in these negotiations, because if one country asked for too high a percentage, Apple could just go elsewhere.

So now we had a situation where companies were paying minuscule amounts, if anything, in taxes abroad. As the *New York Times* reported in late 2017, Apple had been storing cash on the tiny island of Jersey, in the English Channel, which doesn't tax corporate income at all. According to the *Times*, "tax strategies like the ones used by Apple—as well as Amazon, Google, Starbucks and others—cost governments around the world as much as $240 billion in lost revenue." Apple alone was keeping $300 *billion* in cash overseas.

You can't blame these companies for not wanting to pay taxes on that money; from a pure business standpoint, it makes no sense to do so. Yet, at the same time, they would prefer to have their cash back in the United States; otherwise, they have to borrow money in order to cover their expenses and payroll. Some executives were admirably frank about the huge inefficiencies built into this tax code. Apple CEO Tim Cook, for one, came to the U.S. Congress and urged lawmakers to change the system, even if it resulted in Apple's paying more tax.

After studying this tricky problem, I soon came to believe that the question was obvious: How could we make it worth those companies' while to bring their money back to the United States? I decided to approach the problem as an entrepreneur. I would try to come up with a solution that would give all sides a win.

THE CHALLENGE I SET MYSELF WAS THIS: IF WE COULD FIGURE out a way for these companies not to have to pay taxes but rather, to put their overseas cash to good use here at home, we might be able to persuade them to repatriate their money. And the best option, I decided, would be to creatively tie it to an infrastructure program, which would ultimately benefit everyone.

Crafting the right legislation around this idea was no easy task. My first iteration of the bill was this: if companies agreed to invest in newly issued infrastructure bonds, they could bring back a certain amount of their overseas cash tax-free. If, for example, they bought $1 billion in bonds, they could repatriate $4 billion. The bonds would pay zero interest for fifty years; ordinarily that would be a terrible investment option, except that in this case it would be coupled with a big tax break.

We pushed the plan a step further when I came up with an idea for fixing the imbalance between international tax rates. We would create a minimum tax rate for companies to pay on earnings each year, with no option to defer those payments until future years. Companies that required physical presences in international locations, such as Starbucks in Germany, would owe little to no taxes beyond what they'd already paid to those host countries. But a company that was based on intellectual property and that stored its cash in places such as Jersey or other offshore locales would be required to pay the minimum tax to the U.S. government whether or not it chose to bring its money back.

This framework accomplished two things. By our estimates, $1 trillion would come back into the United States practically overnight—essentially a stimulus program that we wouldn't have to pay for—and we would generate about $200 billion in new revenues for the government, of which we would allocate 100 percent to infrastructure. Our plan for spending the revenues was twofold: the federal government would create an infrastructure bank for state and local governments, and it would also increase the funding of the Highway Trust Fund. Combined, this would represent an investment of $1 trillion in infrastructure and create up to ten million jobs over the next ten years—all of it fully paid for.

I believed that if I could just sit down with enough members of Congress, show them my presentation, and explain how this infrastructure bill creatively solved several problems at once, we could get the bipartisan support we needed. So I got out there and did it. I spent countless hours trudging all over Capitol Hill, making my pitch. Soon after my swearing in, I had run to be one of the presidents of my freshman class in Congress and was selected, but that was a piece of cake compared to the legwork involved in drumming up support for this bill.

Slowly but surely, we started getting interest. Along the way, I learned some of the quirks of legislating. A couple of members asked for odd favors in exchange for their support—one told me he'd sign on if I joined his new workout group; another invited me to a 6:00 a.m. football practice on the National Mall, where I managed to lock down another four votes; another listened intently to my pitch and then said, "I don't really understand most of what you just said, but it sounds good. Sign me up." Once we'd broken the dam and gotten the first cosponsor, the rest started coming more easily.

I had first floated the idea of the bill in February 2013, one month after I was sworn in. By the time we introduced it in May, we had thirteen Democrats and thirteen Republicans as cosponsors. Those numbers kept growing, and in the end we had more than forty Democrats and forty Republicans. When I started out, nobody believed we could get anywhere near that kind of bipartisan support, particularly for a bill with a huge tax change and a $1 trillion spending program. Tax and spending policies set off some of the most partisan battles on Capitol Hill, but to the shock of many seasoned Capitol Hill people we did it. And we had support across the ideological spectrum, from members of the Progressive Caucus all the way to the then head of the superconservative Freedom Caucus.

In 2013, this was the biggest bipartisan tax-and-spending bill in Congress, and it would have created a win for both parties as well as for the American people. Unfortunately, however, partisanship won out. Later that year, my bill was held up by the Republican leadership, who wanted to wait for the chance to pass their bigger tax reform bill, which they finally did in 2017.

Yet while the GOP's 2017 tax bill succeeded in fulfilling my goal of persuading companies to repatriate millions, it failed to do anything with that cash other than pay for deep, financially irresponsible tax cuts. Whereas my bill would have improved infrastructure and provided a long-term boost to our economy, the Republicans' bill does neither. In the end, the GOP squandered an opportunity to solve real problems with a workable bipartisan solution—and the American people are the ones who will pay for it.

WHILE IT'S EASY TO ASSUME THAT I'M A BIG FAN OF THIS infrastructure bill because it's my own, others have gotten excited about it as well. Here are just two examples.

First, one morning in 2017, I was reading through the daily briefing from my staff on my iPhone when I did a double take, my eye caught by a headline about a dozen stories down. *Fortune* magazine had named the "World's 50 Greatest Leaders," and among such luminaries as Pope Francis, Jeff Bezos, and Angela Merkel, there was my name, at number thirteen. I had had no idea this was coming, but the accompanying text made it clear that my bipartisan infrastructure bill was the reason I'd been recognized. As the magazine put it:

> As the acerbity of political discourse threatens to infect the whole culture, the best leaders stay refreshingly open to other views, engaging opponents constructively rather than waging war. Republican Gov. John Kasich of Ohio and Democratic Rep. John Delaney of Maryland, for example, advocate

positions the other party favors—and both won reelection easily the last time they faced their home voters. . . .

Being a House Democrat in a government Republicans dominate entirely sounds like a recipe for irrelevance. But one of the new administration's signature issues, rebuilding the nation's infrastructure, is a problem Delaney has focused on since he arrived in Congress four years ago. Delaney is pushing a business-friendly solution: He wants to tap proceeds from repatriated foreign profits to seed public-private partnerships that will take on new projects. That may be the best option for unleashing major spending without blowing a hole in the federal deficit.

Second, it's worth noting that a number of new members of Congress, both Democrats and Republicans, have told me they campaigned on my bill when they were running, telling constituents that if they got into office they would support it. These were candidates I had never met or even heard of; they just believed their constituents were eager for bipartisan solutions, so they embraced my infrastructure bill as a way of gaining support.

People want their elected officials to get things done, and the only real way to do that in an almost evenly divided government is through bipartisan legislation. A party's political base and its hard-core activists may not applaud bipartisanship, but the vast majority of people—everyone in the middle—strongly supports it. Look at the reaction in September 2017, when Chuck Schumer and Nancy Pelosi cut their deal with President Trump to fund the government temporarily and raise the debt ceiling: people were ecstatic that the two parties were working together to get something done.

Bipartisan legislation also has a better of chance of succeeding over the long term. When Congress is able to reach policy agreements with both sides participating, Democrats and Republicans alike are more invested in ensuring that a bill passes the test of time. Legislation that's prepared on a strict party-line basis, however, as we've seen time and time again, tends not to live a long and healthy life. Even if this kind of bill manages to pass, it remains a target for the party that opposed it.

Obamacare is a perfect example. That law passed on a party-line vote, and ever since, the Republicans have fought tooth and nail to get rid of it. It's almost comical; they blame it for absolutely everything that's going wrong. Why is the economy not growing? The Affordable Care Act. Why do we have an opioid crisis? The Affordable Care Act. The Republicans, as a matter of politics, decided to make opposition to this law a centerpiece of their party. They want it dead and buried.

Health care represents one-sixth of the U.S. economy; if that segment of our economy were its own country, it would be one of the largest in the world. As everyone who's ever tried to understand it knows, health care is a hugely complex issue with multiple layers, so if you're going to reform it, you're probably not going to get it entirely right the first time. The best way to manage the implementation of the ACA would have been to get the law passed and then be vigilant about the parts of it that turned out not to work so that we could continue to improve it incrementally. But because of hyperpartisanship, we did none of that.

The ACA, in my view, has two good parts and one good idea implemented badly. The first good part is that it has expanded Medicaid by broadening the eligibility criteria, which a majority of states accepted. Most of the people who've gotten health care under the ACA after previously not having it—meaning, for the most part, some of our poorest citizens—were able to do so because of this Medicaid expansion. That was a tremendously important and successful outcome, but it's not enough. I believe that health care is a right, and ultimately we should move to a system where every American gets a basic package like Medicaid, and the ability to buy private health insurance if they so choose. This system, when combined with Medicare, could allow us to achieve the goal of universal health care in a fiscally responsible way, particularly if it were combined with steps to decouple health care from employment, which currently creates all kinds of bad incentives.

The second good part of the ACA consists of adjustments that were made to improve coverage and change incentives. One excellent example is the rule that people with preexisting conditions can no longer be excluded from coverage. Another is establishing penalties for hospitals that constantly readmit people. Some hospitals had become like health care mills, admitting and readmitting patients without making any real effort to find lower-cost solutions, such as home care or nursing homes. The ACA changes the way hospitals get paid for such treatments, which has led to greater efficiencies and lower costs. Unfortunately, the endless partisan warfare over the bill means that it has never been given proper credit for the undeniable fact that it has lowered the trajectory of health care costs, which is likely to have more influence on our nation's long-term fiscal health than any other factor.

The crucial mistake made when drafting the ACA was the way the health care exchanges were structured. Under the ACA, if you're individually insured, or uninsured, and you don't qualify for Medicaid, you can buy insurance on the exchange. The theory behind this approach, which is based on an idea from Mitt

Romney, is sound. It's the same theory that underlies all insurance, which is that if you pool people together, you can spread the risk in a way that makes it possible for everyone to get a good deal and not get excluded based on health conditions.

Here's the problem, though: in an effort to protect people between the ages of fifty-five and sixty-five, the ACA mandated that the exchanges could charge them only up to three times the cost of the cheapest policy on offer. Did someone forget to do the math? Health care costs for people in that age range are, on average, *six times* what they are for young, healthy people.

In our free-market system, an insurance company running an exchange had to find a way to make up for the losses it absorbed on the fifty-five- to sixty-five-year-olds in its plan. Its solution was simple: it raised the premiums on everyone else. Not surprisingly, the younger and healthier people weren't happy about the high premiums, so many of them either sought coverage elsewhere or simply dropped their plan and paid the penalty mandated by the ACA. Caught between the two extremes were middle-aged people, often with young children, who needed coverage but had no better options. Before long, they were getting crushed by the escalating premium costs.

So how can we fix this problem? Some people argue that we should charge the market rate for all those people between fifty-five and sixty-five who are getting a great deal. But there's a better way. My solution would be to let people over fifty-five buy into Medicare. Right now, people sixty-five and over are eligible for Medicare, and they get it for free. Why not change the rules so that people between fifty-five and sixty-five pay the same amount in fees they're paying now, but for coverage through Medicare? They'd still get a good deal, the exchanges wouldn't be hamstrung, and Medicare is large enough to absorb the costs associated with covering all these new people. This approach will make the individual markets much healthier, lower premiums for younger participants, and boost enrollment.

To help pay for the costs involved in this shift to Medicare, I would allow the government to negotiate pricing with pharmaceutical companies on drugs purchased for Medicare. Think about it: one the largest purchasers of medications on the planet, the U.S. government, cannot negotiate the prices for the drugs it buys. This is utterly ridiculous; can you imagine how Walmart would respond if told it couldn't negotiate prices with its suppliers? But thanks to relentless lobbying by powerful drug companies, that's the situation we find ourselves in. As a result, the government is transferring billions of dollars each year from the American taxpayer to the shareholders of pharmaceutical companies.

This scandalous arrangement is unacceptable, and the sooner we change it, the better. We should also add more "pay for results only" regimes for newly innovative, very expensive drugs. This would allow for a handsome payment if a drug worked on a patient, and nothing if it didn't. Finally, I would also add a public option to the health care exchanges so that people had more choices available to them when selecting an insurance plan.

Health care is so complicated that we simply must have bipartisan discussion on the issue. It is the single most important variable in our long-term fiscal health as a nation. Both Democrats and Republicans must be in the room—no more secret discussions behind closed doors, rushed votes, or a sense that one party is trying to put something over on the other. And when we negotiate with our colleagues on the other side of the table, we have to remember that health care is finally about three things: access, cost, and quality. Beyond fixing the Affordable Care Act, any comprehensive reform has to address all three.

LET'S PULL BACK FROM SPECIFIC LEGISLATION AND ADDRESS another question. It's easy enough to say that the two parties should work together and that we should craft solutions that take into account the different sides' opinions. Over the past few years, though, both parties have been becoming increasingly partisan. Instead of moving toward the middle, we've been racing in opposite directions. What makes me think that I can turn that tide?

I'm betting on bipartisanship because it's the right answer to the tremendous problems we're facing today. And I'm stating my belief in bipartisan governance clearly, right at the outset, so there's no question as to what I stand for. If the American people choose to elect me as president, they will be giving me an unmistakable mandate to do everything possible to ensure that Democrats and Republicans work together. This is the only way we can overcome the obstructionist nature of whichever party is in the minority, and we simply must get both sides to buy in to the idea.

If I am elected president, I will immediately take three concrete steps to foster bipartisan communication and cooperation.

1. Focus only on bipartisan bills in the first one hundred days

My career in business taught me that the tone at the top matters. How you lead, the kind of fingerprints you leave on your actions, the messages you send to those who work for you—all these signals tell people a great deal about how you expect them to act.

As president, I would commit to prioritizing only bipartisan ideas during my first one hundred days in office. We need to learn how to accomplish things together again, and this action would send a message to the American people, and the Congress, that the time for fighting is over. The promises that candidates make when outlining their plans for the first one hundred days often reflect partisan priorities, initiatives they will undertake over the strong objections of the other party. Yet that approach sets the stage for a presidency rooted in opposition. Instead, our next president's first order of business must be to end the partisan division and make every effort to unite the country.

2. Have a daily breakfast with members of Congress

If you spend any amount of time on Capitol Hill, you will soon hear someone reminiscing about the good old days, when Democrats and Republicans used to have meals, play golf, and generally socialize together. In past decades, legislators had relationships that went beyond seeing each other in the Capitol, and there wasn't any stigma attached to having a friendly chat with someone from the other party.

These days, there seems to be an unwritten rule that the two sides shouldn't mix. Newer members of Congress don't really know the people on the other side of the aisle, and that hurts the legislative process. How can we work together to solve America's problems if we can't even have conversations with each other?

As president, I would have a member of Congress over for breakfast every morning. If that sounds like overkill, it's not. Here's how we'd set up these meetings.

The breakfast would start at 8:00 a.m., in the room right next to the Oval Office. For the first fifteen minutes, my chief of staff would sit down with the guest and invite him or her to vent, make a proposal, or simply talk through whatever it was he or she wanted me to know. I would arrive at 8:15, my chief of staff would leave, and then the congressional member and I would have breakfast together, during which I'd ask about that person's life. Given that I would expect to be dealing with this member of Congress, I would want to actually get to know him or her.

At the end of breakfast, I would ask, "What can I do to help you?" And the member could tell me or ask me anything, knowing that I would keep our conversation private. After that, my chief of staff would come back in and the three of us would discuss whether there was anything on which we needed to follow up.

If we did this every day that Congress was in session, I would ultimately have a chance to meet every member, whether Democrat or Republican. I'm sure that in some instances we would discover areas of mutual interest that could help move along some legislation. And throughout this process, I would undoubtedly develop personal relationships with some of the members. With a little luck, I'd also win some goodwill that would help smooth relations more generally.

3. Address the caucuses once a quarter and hold regular town halls with citizens

Every week, the Democrats and Republicans in Congress meet together in a caucus, where they hash out ideas and make plans for the week ahead. As president, I would make a point of joining these meetings once each quarter, essentially saying, "Here I am. I'm listening. Let's talk." I would also plan to spend at least part of that day in the Presidents Room, a rarely used ceremonial office in the Capitol Building, during which I would meet with small groups of congressmen and -women to discuss ways we could work together. I would also hold town halls twice a year, with bipartisan audiences, not just supporters. This would be my way of leading by example, of showing that we can once again sit down together and have meaningful discussions about what we agree on and what we don't.

These solutions may sound elementary, but I believe they would have a profound impact on the atmosphere in the Capitol. One of the biggest problems of hyperpartisanship is that everybody feels like the other side isn't listening. We don't have to air our differences through Twitter, or on the cable television shows, or via proxies. That hasn't worked, so it's time to return to a simpler, more humane strategy. We need to look the other person in the eye, listen carefully to what he or she is saying, and do our best to understand points of view that differ from our own. We've forgotten how to talk to each other, and it's time we remembered the value of genuine dialogue.

CHAPTER 3

Open the Door

A wise government seeks to provide the opportunity
through which the best of individual achievement
can be obtained . . .

FRANKLIN DELANO ROOSEVELT

IT WAS A CHILLY, CLEAR MORNING IN DECEMBER 1998 WHEN
I made my way to the Financial District of Manhattan for a special honor. At thirty-five years old, I was about to become the
youngest CEO of a company on the New York Stock Exchange
when HealthCare Financial Partners began trading on the exchange.
And on this bright winter morning, I was heading to the NYSE's
stately building on Broad Street for the honor of ringing the
opening bell on the trading floor.

On my way there, I took a moment to look across the spar-
kling waters of the Hudson River. To the south, I could see the
Statue of Liberty and, off to her side, the low-slung buildings of
Ellis Island, where Albert Rowe had arrived seventy-four years

before. I sometimes get a little choked up when looking at these landmarks of American history, but on that day I was thinking about another place, one that had also played an important role in my life. It was an unexceptional building nestled across the river in Jersey City, New Jersey: the former home of the Union Hall for International Brotherhood of Electrical Workers, Local 164.

IBEW 164 was my dad's union, which included a couple thousand electricians from northern New Jersey. Members of Local 164 had electrified some of the biggest projects in the region: the Lincoln and Holland Tunnels, the Meadowlands sports facilities, the George Washington Bridge. My dad was a union guy to the core; he loved the brotherhood and appreciated the protections the union gave him. When I was finishing my senior year of high school in 1981, his union stepped up to help me, too, offering a scholarship that would enable me to go to college.

Wood-Ridge was a small town of Irish, Polish, and Italian immigrant families, and, like me, most of the kids I knew there had working-class parents. My father would have been happy if I'd followed in his footsteps as an electrician, but my mother had a different dream for me. She had always urged me to get an education—in particular, she wanted me to go to college and become a doctor, like my uncle Jack.

John "Jack" Rowe is my mother's brother, the only son of Albert Rowe. He's a medical doctor, but he's also one of the most creative thinkers in the field of health care. In his late twenties, he became the founding director of the Division of Aging at Harvard, where he essentially founded the field of gerontology. He went on to become the chief of gerontology at Beth Israel Hospital in Boston, and then the head of Mount Sinai–New York University Medical Center and Health System, and then the CEO and chairman of Aetna. By any measure, he has had a tremendously impressive career. But to me, as a young boy in suburban New Jersey, he was just Uncle Jack.

When I was growing up, Jack lived in Boston, so I would see him only a few times a year, but when I did, I'd always take the opportunity to ask his advice. As I got older, he became a mentor, and I made a habit of running most of my big decisions by him. I remember seeing him over Thanksgiving break during my senior year in high school and giving him my college application essay to read. I was a little nervous, partly because I'd written that although I was planning on studying science, I wasn't sure exactly what I wanted to do. He told me he liked the essay, which was a relief, and then recommended that I revise the opening line to say that my career plans were "incompletely formulated." That sounded great to me, so I made the change and submitted my application. Within a few months, I was proud and excited to receive my letter of acceptance to Columbia University.

Uncle Jack gave me advice on how to get into Columbia, and the IBEW scholarship made it possible for me to actually go there. So, once a year, for each of the four years I was in college, I would go across the river for an evening meeting at IBEW 164 in Jersey City. While the electricians ate sandwiches and drank beer, I'd walk onto the stage in front of the room and give a little speech, thanking them for my scholarship. I always felt nervous before my talk, but they invariably gave me a warm welcome, and I left those meetings feeling grateful all over again for the generosity displayed by the hardworking union members who reached into their paychecks each week to make it possible for me to attend Columbia.

Although I ultimately decided not to study medicine, my

college education served as a springboard to later success, which in turn gave me the opportunity to pursue my dream of becoming an entrepreneur, which led, eventually, to that morning in 1998 when I rang the bell at the NYSE. I worked hard to build my company and achieve that honor, and over the years some people have described me as a "self-made man." Yet the truth is there is no such thing. I couldn't have done it without the support of mentors, countless teachers along the way, and the help of people such as the members of the IBEW brotherhood. If they had not opened the door of opportunity for me, my life would have turned out very differently.

No one navigates the challenges of life alone. Each night, on my way from the U.S. Capitol to my home in Maryland, I drive across the Arlington Memorial Bridge and onto the George Washington Parkway in Virginia. Crossing the bridge, I can see straight into Arlington National Cemetery, where thousands of heroes are buried. At that moment, I often think about those who made the ultimate sacrifice to give us all the opportunities we have. In light of the gift given to us by these patriots, how can anyone believe that he or she has achieved success without help? It is by the grace and generosity of those brave men and women that we are living in the land of the free.

THIS IS THE ESSENCE OF THE AMERICAN DREAM: THAT someone like me, the son of an electrician, the grandson of a dockworker and pencil factory employee, can achieve the kind of personal and financial success my immigrant forebears came here to seek. It's a classic story, the kind immortalized by my favorite songwriter, Bruce Springsteen, whose lyrics so beautifully capture the struggles of ordinary people seeking better lives. But my fear is that, with the way things are going now, fewer and fewer young Americans will have this kind of opportunity.

Today, almost two-thirds of Americans under the age of eighteen are growing up in places where there's no upward economic mobility. These are the hollowed-out towns and inner cities where the economy is in tatters, wages are stagnant, families are struggling, and life expectancy is going down, in part because of the opioid epidemic ravaging our country. These are places where people go to bed each night worrying about how they will support their families, where basic human dignity has been stripped away by lack of opportunity. It's incredibly hard to escape the cycle of poverty in such places. There, the American dream feels out of reach, leading kids to believe they can't escape their fates and dooming too many of them to life at the poverty line.

One afternoon a few years ago, a high school student from Cumberland, Maryland, visited my congressional office. The Cumberland metropolitan area, which has much higher than average rates of poverty and unemployment, is a former industrial hub at the edge of the Appalachian Mountains that's been struggling significantly for the last several decades. But this young man had won a statewide math award, and because Maryland boasts many very high ranked high schools, this meant he was truly exceptional at math.

We talked for a bit in my office, and I asked him where he planned to go to college. Given that he'd won this prestigious award, I expected him to say he'd chosen to go to an elite university, perhaps M.I.T. or an Ivy League school, or that he'd been given a full scholarship to, say, Johns Hopkins in Baltimore. Instead, he told me he was planning to go to a small public college not far from his home. This was a solid school that does a good job of serving its community, but I doubted that its math and engineering curriculum would truly challenge a brilliant math student such as this young man.

When I asked him why he'd chosen that particular college, he said simply, "Because it's close by." It's possible that he had worthy reasons to want to stay close to home—perhaps an ailing parent, or a sibling who needed him, or any of a hundred other possibilities—but his answer made me wonder whether the reasoning behind his decision had come, at least in part, out of the environment in which he'd been raised. Like so many kids from these depressed areas, he had most likely grown up having no expectation that he'd ever get out. And if that was the case, it was clearly having an impact on his future.

Over the years, I've met a number of other high school students who never even dreamed of going to any college far from home. That's a huge loss to our communities and our country. So how can we help ensure that students, no matter their background, are maximizing their opportunities? One way is through innovative programs such as the academy set up by Northwestern University in 2013.

Chicago public schools have a magnet program for the city's most promising students, but those magnet schools can take only so many of them. To be eligible, students have to achieve a certain score on a standardized test; then, to be granted admission from that pool, they have to win a computerized lottery. The random nature of the lottery means that many qualified students get left out in the cold. Northwestern, under its president, Morton Schapiro, responded to this problem by creating the Northwestern Academy for Chicago Public Schools, which was designed to educate the high-achieving kids who weren't lucky enough to win the lottery.

Northwestern Academy, which offers both academic year and summer programs, has a simple mission: "To increase access and the successful matriculation of underrepresented and talented Chicago Public Schools students to top-tier colleges and universities by providing college preparation programming, academic support and enrichment, self-regulatory learning experiences, and nurturing aspirations."

It's that last phrase, "nurturing aspirations," that hints at the deeper roots of the program. In greenlighting the academy, Schapiro hoped to encourage students from less upwardly mobile communities to aim higher academically. When I asked about the idea behind the academy, he told me that he'd always wanted to attract more lower-income students to Northwestern, but too few applied, either because of the social stigma among their peers or because they didn't believe they could afford it. Instead, high-achieving lower-income students would pay to go to community colleges even though Northwestern and others are eager to enroll them and would provide them a full scholarship.

Northwestern Academy solved that problem by funneling high school kids into an academically challenging and supportive environment from the ninth grade on, thus lifting their expectations about what was possible and how much they were capable of accomplishing. These are exactly the kinds of out-of-the-box programs we should be developing. As someone who benefited enormously from a helping hand when he was young, I strongly believe that it's our obligation to help students recognize and pursue the myriad opportunities available to them.

WE CAN'T WAIT UNTIL STUDENTS REACH HIGH SCHOOL before helping them, however. We've got to start when they are very young, with pre-kindergarten (pre-K) education. The current data on children and education overwhelmingly suggest that providing pre-K for kids is one of the best investments we can make, because it changes the entire trajectory of their K–12 educational experience. Kids who go to pre-K are more prepared for school, they tend to score higher on tests than those who don't, and they're only half as likely to end up in special-needs programs down the road. Significantly, pre-K helps children from poor and disadvantaged backgrounds succeed. And pre-K particularly helps kids from bilingual backgrounds, such as those from Hispanic or other immigrant families, to improve their academic performance.

Pre-K has been on the rise for years, but we're still a long way from full government funding, which should be our ultimate goal. Until we get there, innovative leaders will continue to search for other ways to provide this invaluable program. One such leader, Salt Lake County mayor Ben McAdams, implemented a creative solution to the problem that other cities would do well to emulate.

Mayor McAdams didn't have enough money in his budget for universal pre-K, so he turned to so-called impact investors, philanthropists and foundations who invest with the goal of a social (as opposed to financial) return. The arrangement he made comprised several steps. First, the investors would fund universal pre-K. Then, the children's educational development would be continually measured for several years as they progressed through school. Finally, if these students ended up requiring less special-needs education as a result of pre-K, the government would make a "success payment," that is, a payment to investors with a small rate of return—one it could afford thanks to the money saved from spending less on the far more costly special-ed programs.

These kinds of arrangements involve a particular kind of impact investing called Pay for Success financing, which I'll discuss later at greater length. The upshot is they deliver three clear benefits: the government saves money, the impact investors eventually get their donations back (which are then recycled into more social impact projects), and the children enjoy greater academic success. Win-win-win.

Pay for Success is a great way to solve a number of the problems we face, but it won't solve the problem of how to fund universal pre-K, as it would take a lot of time to get cities, towns, and communities across the country on board. I believe we need universal pre-K right now, and the best way to achieve this would be with full funding from the federal government. Yet, as with so many issues, Democrats and Republicans strongly disagree on how to go forward, so I have a plan for meeting in the middle—not a mushy compromise, but a way to help make it happen by providing wins for both sides.

How do we do that? Republicans tend to feel that parents don't have enough choice in schools and that the school system we run now is too expensive. They have a point, particularly with respect to pre-K. There's a significant cost differential between building universal pre-K within the public education system and providing funding to leverage existing community-based programs.

The way pre-K works now isn't terribly efficient. In addition to pre-K programs in traditional public schools, there are numerous small community-based programs that tend to be close to people's homes and workplaces. These are popular because, in most cases, parents' biggest concern is finding a pre-K nearby, as preschool kids are often too young to take school buses. So when Republicans say they'd prefer such community-based programs over building pre-K into existing schools, there's good reason to listen to them and weave this into a compromise. Besides, we don't need to build a whole new pre-K system. At least half the infrastructure we need already exists in programs such as Montessori and Head Start and in church-based programs. In addition, many successful and high-performing charter schools are expanding into pre-K, which is even more good news.

Many Democrats, however, would prefer expanding the public schools to include pre-K classrooms. But we simply don't have enough money to do that—not even close. It would cost much more to build those new classrooms in our schools than it would to use existing community structures.

I believe that the best way to create universal pre-K quickly and in a bipartisan manner is for the federal government to provide block grants (with states providing matching grants) that would fund one year of pre-K for every four-year-old in each state either in a traditional public school or through a community-based program. And although pre-K would be free and available to every family, it would not be mandatory. I'm convinced that most states would take that offer in a heartbeat.

To pay for the plan, I would propose a modest tax on the income of very wealthy Americans, to be structured as a new revenue stream that would be walled off from the general budget of the United States. In this case, the concept of dedicated revenues makes sense, as it would force elected officials to sell the merits of this specific program, as opposed to simply raising taxes and dropping the extra revenue into what many Americans view as the black hole of the federal budget. True, no one likes new taxes, but it's important to note that many wealthy Americans already allocate philanthropic giving to early childhood education. They understand the benefits to society and rightly view it as a very high return on investment.

In this way, we can come together around a bipartisan plan to fully fund free pre-K education. Both Republicans and Democrats can claim a win—and children will benefit.

PROVIDING UNIVERSAL PRE-K IS A GREAT WAY TO ENSURE that American kids start off their schooling on the right foot. But what happens at the other end of their educational experience? When American students emerge from the K–12 system, many go off to college. But what about those who don't? Are they prepared to enter the job market? Increasingly, the answer to that question seems to be no. Why is that? And how can we fix it?

In several European countries, students get tracked into vocational training even before they reach high school. French students, for example, are divided in their early teens into one group that will continue academic study and another that will be shifted to a vocational high school. The vocational students take specialized courses to learn hands-on skills such as plumbing, carpentry, and welding. If all goes well, they can enter seamlessly into the workforce as soon as they graduate high school.

In our country we take a different approach, for a couple of reasons. First, we're uncomfortable with the idea of telling a ninth-grader that he or she won't be going to college. It feels antithetical to our American ideals, which hold that children can grow up to become anything they want to be. Second, our public school system is a massively decentralized operation, run by thousands of local school boards, which means that even if we wanted to switch to a French-style vocational system, actually accomplishing this would be all but impossible.

Still, if we can't offer free vocational training through our public high schools, we can do the next best thing. We can offer all high school graduates free community college or vocational certificate training.

I believe that every young person in this country has a basic right to education, and that shouldn't stop at high school graduation, particularly because a high school diploma no longer has much meaning in today's job market. Community colleges can provide a crucial lifeline for young adults trying to find their way into meaningful employment. Numerous rewarding jobs, ranging from dental hygienist to radiology technician to paralegal, require only two-year associate degrees, and many of these jobs pay upwards of $75,000 a year. The more young adults we can get into these kinds of jobs, the more competitive our country will be.

This program will require investment, but there are existing public-private partnerships we can use as models, such as apprenticeship programs run by building trades unions, and partnerships between businesses and local community colleges in which education is designed to train students for skilled-labor jobs that local businesses are trying to fill. Another aspect of the program would involve "student grants" that would go only to schools that can show that the vast majority of their graduates find employment in their fields, because when we talk about taking on new expenditures of this size, results matter.

When young people can't find work after twelve years of schooling, they suffer, and the country suffers, too. At the end of 2017, U.S. companies had *six million* jobs they couldn't fill because they weren't able to find qualified workers. Yet even at a moment when our nation's unemployment rate is remarkably low, millions of high school graduates still can't find good jobs. That's an unacceptable state of affairs.

This skills gap, as it's called, is a huge problem in our country, and it's likely to grow. Yet even though all sides agree that we need to close that gap, we've done absolutely nothing about it. Some who've studied this problem believe we should create public-private partnerships for workforce training, and such solutions can be essentially bipartisan. But these ideas aren't particularly innovative, which is one reason Congress hasn't yet supported them.

Can we find a creative new way to close this skills gap? I believe we can, and we should do it by reintroducing national service and combining it with an apprenticeship program. Plans like this one, admittedly, are not new—similar initiatives have been proposed by Gen. Stanley McChrystal and businessman James Stone—but the basic idea is that young Americans would fulfill either one year of paid community service or two years of military service, usually after graduating from high school. The approach to community service would be similar to that offered by AmeriCorps, which employs seventy-five thousand Americans in jobs such as disaster services, education, and environmental stewardship. AmeriCorps and programs like it—Teach For America and the Peace Corps come to mind—provide a fantastic way for young people to get hands-on job experience and do some good for the country before moving on to further pursue their education or careers.

In addition to the military and community service branches of national service, we should set up a third branch, focused on infrastructure. This would be a public-private partnership in which private companies were awarded contracts to undertake projects such as improving public parks or renovating federal buildings to make them environmentally green. We should involve the trade unions whenever possible, leveraging their successful apprenticeship program model. Young people who signed up for the infrastructure branch would be apprenticed to these private companies. They'd work with the companies' employees to learn the skills needed to complete these projects and would receive a certificate when their service was complete. This opportunity would be introduced to students during high school as part of a new civics and financial literacy curriculum that I would propose—something we desperately need, as our democracy is under threat both from extreme partisanship and, as we saw in the 2016 election, from outside forces.

Most of the benefits generated by programs like this one are obvious. The certificate the apprentices received attesting to their skills training would help them move on to better work after their service, the companies would get apprentice labor to help with their projects, and public areas and buildings would be improved. It's another win-win-win, the best kind of project.

Then there are the less obvious, but equally important, benefits. Programs like this one would bring about tremendous social and economic mixing. Decades ago, people from all walks of life served in the military, which helped make it a powerful unifying force in American society. Today, that benefit is lost to most of us, other than the patriotic young men and women who join our armed services. The opportunities for people from starkly different socioeconomic classes to meet and get to know one another have therefore diminished dramatically. National service would go a long way toward restoring this kind of unifying experience.

Because there's no real mechanism for making national service mandatory, nor public support for it, we would need to be creative in finding ways to get young people involved. I have some ideas for how to do that.

For many young people, the notion of spending the year right after high school working and developing skills would be payoff enough; it could serve as a "gap year," an increasingly popular choice among college-bound high school graduates. To encourage young people to sign up for national service, I would take this idea a step further, incentivizing colleges to favor admitting students who have fulfilled their national service. One way to accomplish this would be to follow the template of the National Minimum Drinking Age Act, which President Ronald Reagan signed into law in 1984.

In 1980, different states had different minimum drinking ages, which ranged anywhere from eighteen to twenty-one. That year, a California teenager named Cari Lightner was killed in a tragic drunk-driving accident. In response, her bereaved mother, Candace, created Mothers Against Drunk Driving, which quickly became a powerful force in Washington. Eager to reduce drunk-driving deaths, MADD spearheaded a movement to raise the minimum drinking age to twenty-one nationwide. Yet there was no mechanism for doing that nationally, as each state still had the right to determine its own drinking age.

In 1984, Democratic senator Frank Lautenberg of New Jersey found a way around the problem. He wrote a law that essentially incentivized states to raise their minimum drinking ages by tying the issue to federal highway funds. States could still choose to maintain their lower drinking ages, but they would receive 10 percent less federal funding. Every state in the union ultimately decided to raise the minimum age, and today you must be twenty-one to drink anywhere in the United States.

To make national service work, we would need to encourage students to sign up for the program and colleges to support it. One way to do this would be to discount the interest rates or balances on student loans for those who served. Another, which I've already hinted at, would be to link federal funding for a university to a requirement that a certain percentage of the students it accepted be those who have completed their national service.

For the infrastructure branch, we would start by requiring all federal contractors to design and implement an apprentice program. Next, we would encourage other companies to do their patriotic duty and follow suit, perhaps using a model that's been tremendously successful in Switzerland, where companies pay students to work as part-time apprentices. Finally, we would market this program to high school graduates as an opportunity to serve their country, travel, get paid while learning a skill, and earn a certificate.

These proposals may seem drastic, but the skills gap in our country is huge and growing, and the divisions it creates are an even bigger problem. If our young people aren't prepared for the workforce, we will not continue to thrive as a nation. Our government must take steps to help young Americans learn the skills needed to support themselves, fill our millions of job vacancies, and make our country stronger by working together.

ON JUNE 27, 1936, FRANKLIN DELANO ROOSEVELT GAVE A speech accepting his nomination as the Democratic candidate for the presidency. Roosevelt was just finishing his first term, having led the nation during its tumultuous recovery from the Great Depression.

When FDR first took office in 1933, millions of Americans were homeless and millions more unemployed. The stock market had cratered, and American industries were devastated. In the first one hundred days of his administration, Roosevelt launched what became the First New Deal, promoting and ultimately signing a remarkable package of legislation that put the nation back on its feet. The list of programs he started is astonishing: the Federal Deposit Insurance Corporation (FDIC), the Securities and Exchange Commission (SEC), the Federal Communications Commission (FCC), the Public Works Administration (PWA), and the Civilian Conservation Corps (CCC) were all created during Roosevelt's first term.

Thanks in large part to Roosevelt's leadership, by 1936 the country had begun the difficult process of pulling itself out of the mire. But as Roosevelt pointed out in his speech at the Democratic National Convention, the nascent recovery had created other problems, some of them serious.

Primary among them was a growing inequality between rich and poor. In his speech, Roosevelt raised the alarm about the "economic royalists" who sought to prevent government from helping those in need.

For too many of us the political equality we once had won was meaningless in the face of economic inequality. A small group had concentrated into their own hands an almost complete control over other people's property, other people's money, other people's labor—other people's lives. For too many of us life was no longer free; liberty no longer real; men could no longer follow the pursuit of happiness.

Against economic tyranny such as this, the American citizen could appeal only to the organized power of Government. The collapse of 1929 showed up the despotism for what it was. The election of 1932 was the people's mandate to end it. Under that mandate it is being ended.

The royalists of the economic order have conceded that political freedom was the business of the Government, but they have maintained that economic slavery was nobody's business. They granted that the Government could protect the citizen in his right to vote, but they denied that the Government could do anything to protect the citizen in his right to work and his right to live.

For a leader such as FDR, who had so effectively used the levers of his office to improve the lives of millions of Americans, the notion that government couldn't, or shouldn't, help citizens in need was ludicrous. He completely rejected the idea that government was overstepping its role, declaring, "These economic royalists complain that we seek to overthrow the institutions of America. What they really complain of is that we seek to take away their power."

He then doubled down on his contention that our government should actively help its people, saying:

The brave and clear platform adopted by this Convention, to which I heartily subscribe, sets forth that Government in a modern civilization has certain inescapable obligations to its citizens, among which are protection of the family and the home, the establishment of a democracy of opportunity, and aid to those overtaken by disaster . . .

Better the occasional faults of a Government that lives in a spirit of charity than the consistent omissions of a Government frozen in the ice of its own indifference.

Reading Roosevelt's words, I'm struck by how apt they are today, eight decades after he spoke them. The gap between rich and poor is as vast now as it has ever been, and the belief that our country provides genuine opportunity to working-class Americans is dwindling. Rising inequality has created a crisis for millions of individuals and families and has now put the whole country at risk.

As famed investor Ray Dalio pointed out in a 2017 opinion piece titled "Our Biggest Economic, Social, and Political Issue," the differences between the top 40 percent and the bottom 60 percent are stark. Here are several of the points Dalio made to illustrate the problem.

- The average household in the top 40 percent earns four times more than the average household in the bottom 60 percent.

- Those in the top 40 percent now have on average ten times as much wealth as those in the bottom 60 percent. That is up from six times as much in 1980.

• Only about a third of the bottom 60 percent saves any of its income (in cash or financial assets). As a result, according to a recent Federal Reserve study, most people in this group would struggle to raise four hundred dollars in an emergency.

• Though the bottom 60 percent has a small amount of savings, only a quarter of it is in cash or financial assets; the majority is in much less liquid forms of wealth, such as cars, real estate, and business equity. Also, the debt the bottom carries is skewed toward more expensive student, auto, and credit card debt.

• Retirement savings for the bottom 60 percent are not even close to adequate and haven't much improved as the economy and markets have recovered. Only about a third of families in the bottom 60 percent has retirement savings accounts (e.g., pensions, 401[k]s), which average less than twenty thousand dollars.

• The top 40 percent spends four times more on education than the bottom 60 percent. This creates a self-perpetuating problem, because those at the bottom get a much worse education than those at the top.

These figures suggest a looming national catastrophe and make it painfully clear that, for the bottom 60 percent of our people, the American dream is under siege—particularly for communities of color, where the data are even more troubling.

When I first ran for office, I met with a diverse group of young Democrats. One member of the group was a girl, probably about fifteen or so, who had emigrated as a child with her family from Nigeria. She told me that every morning she and her mother had breakfast together before her mom went to her job as a maid at a hotel chain. "My mother always takes my hand," the girl told me, "and she says, 'Don't worry, my dear. No matter what happens today, everything will be fine, because you are in America—the land of opportunity.'"

Ever since our founding, opening the door to opportunity has played a key role in making us a great and powerful nation. But you shouldn't have to be born into the right family or in the right neighborhood to have a shot at a brighter future in America. We have been and must remain a nation of opportunity, not of birthright. Let's make sure we keep those doors of opportunity open for all our citizens and for the generations of Americans to come.

CHAPTER 4

Harness the Power of Incentives

I think I've been in the top 5% of my age cohort all my life in understanding the power of incentives, and all my life I've underestimated it.

CHARLIE MUNGER

NEITHER OF MY PARENTS ATTENDED COLLEGE, BUT MY mother understood that the way to a better life involved getting a good education, so she pushed me hard to excel in my studies. She's the one who urged me to apply to Columbia University, which had two things going for it. First, it was close to home, a requirement for my parents. And second, my uncle Jack approved of the idea.

From the time I was very young, everyone in my family assumed I would become a doctor like Uncle Jack. So, when I started at Columbia, I declared biology as my major and began taking courses that would prepare me for medical school. I worked in the pediatric emergency room at St. Luke's Hospital and also got to take part in some pioneering research on monoclonal anti-bodies at Columbia-Presbyterian Medical Center. That's when I discovered something surprising. As it turned out, I had absolutely no interest in being a doctor. I didn't feel engaged by the work, and I didn't like being in a hospital.

This presented a real problem. My parents had sacrificed a lot for me to have this opportunity, and I didn't want to let them down. Yet, it also occurred to me that I had never actually chosen to become a doctor; it's just what was always expected. Now that I understood I had a choice, I realized I had no idea what I wanted to do with my life.

During my junior year at Columbia, a roommate of mine named Alex Pitofsky started talking about law school. Alex was from Chevy Chase, Maryland, and I had stayed in his family's home there while visiting Washington, DC, with him a few times. The more Alex talked about law school, the more appealing it sounded, not only because I thought that being a lawyer might be a good career but because I needed some way to reassure my parents that I wasn't going to waste my college education. Saying "I'm not going to be a doctor" doesn't sound nearly as bad when you add "But I'm going to be a lawyer" at the end of it.

I decided to double-major in biology and English, took the LSAT, and applied to just one law school, Georgetown. Fortunately, I was accepted, so I was able to finish Columbia with a whole new plan in mind. Yet even before I attended my first class at Georgetown, I caught a glimpse of something that excited me even more than law school.

During the summers, I would usually work with my dad at his electrical jobs. The summer after I graduated from Columbia, though, I decided to work with a buddy of mine, a guy named

Dominic Tucci. Dominic and I had met a few years earlier, at a gym, and became friends over workouts. His dad had a small excavation business in New Jersey, and Dominic was a bulldozer operator there. The summer before I started law school, I worked for his dad's company as a mason laborer on a construction job in the Meadowlands.

Dominic's dad had a contract with a company called Russo Development, which was owned by Larry Russo, who brought in a lawyer named Frank Reiger as a partner in many of his deals. The company was successful—it built warehouses and did a lot of residential work—and I was intrigued by the fact that a lawyer could be a partner in that kind of business. That summer, while digging ditches and carrying cinder blocks, Dominic and I would talk about what a great deal Russo and Reiger had going. "They do whatever they want," I said to Dominic. "They are their own bosses and don't have to answer to anybody."

That was the kind of job I wanted. So Dominic and I hatched a plan to start our own development company. He would stay in the construction business, I would get my law degree, and we'd start our company and build buildings together in northern New Jersey.

At the time, I knew almost nothing about business. I wasn't one of those kids who spend college summers working at investment banks; I was a blue-collar kid living a blue-collar life. Nobody in my family had ever started or run his own business. All I knew was what little I'd gleaned from working for Dominic's father's company, and that wasn't much. Still, there was something about the notion of starting my own company that seemed exciting. And I suppose I didn't know enough to be scared or unsure about what we were doing.

Dominic was as excited as I was about this idea, and we were eager to get things under way. I decided not to wait until I graduated from law school, so while I was still a first-year student, we went ahead and hatched a plan for our initial project, a real estate deal in my hometown of Wood-Ridge.

We had identified a busy street where some redevelopment was happening, with condominiums and apartment buildings going up. Our goal was to persuade the owners of five contiguous houses to agree to sell us their homes, contingent upon our getting approval to build a twenty-unit, multifamily project on the site. As an incentive for them to sell, we would offer them an amount significantly above the properties' appraised value. We weren't yet sure how we'd get the money to buy the homes and build the new apartment building, but we figured if we could get the home owners to agree to sell, and obtain the necessary zoning approvals, we'd be able to find someone to lend us the money.

We started knocking on doors. Because we were approaching people with no advance notice, I had to figure out quickly how to pitch our idea. (These home owners must have thought it a little odd to find a couple of twenty-two-year-olds sitting in their living rooms trying to persuade them to sell their houses just so we could knock them down.) Even though I'd never done anything like this before, right away I loved the experience of selling an idea. It was exciting and a little nerve-racking, but it was a big thrill when I managed to persuade that first home owner to go along with our plan.

At the same time, I was busy researching the zoning laws of Wood-Ridge. I spent extra hours in the law school library, looking up relevant statutes and filing applications with the zoning board. We hired an architect to work up a sketch of what the new apartment building would look like, and after a lot of those living room meetings, Dominic and I finally had contracts for all five houses in hand. This was it: we had all our ducks in a row. There was just one final step: we had to present our case at a zoning board hearing.

The Wood-Ridge Zoning Board set a date for our hearing and put out a public notice. I bought myself a suit, and on the day of the hearing I drove from Georgetown to New Jersey. Dominic and I had done all our homework, and I hoped this last step would be little more than a formality.

Boy, was I wrong. The local residents came out in droves, and from the moment the hearing began it was obvious that while the town was indifferent to it, the future neighbors of our proposed building didn't like our plan. I tried to argue our case the way a lawyer would, but I was still only a first-year law student, and in the end I got crushed. People spoke out loud and clear against us, completely shutting us down.

Dominic and I lost the vote—and that was the end of our short development career. I drove back down to Georgetown disappointed but not discouraged. If anything, our failed attempt at real estate development had left me even more determined to find a way to succeed as an entrepreneur.

That desire was stoked further during my second year of law school, when I clerked for a small firm that owned a real estate development business on the side. Usually when you clerk for a firm, it's all law all the time. In this case, though, I was able to work on the firm's development business as well, and the more I saw of entrepreneurship, the more I was drawn to it. I liked the independence and the freedom. I liked the notion of building something and the feeling of pride that comes from turning an idea into a reality. I also liked the fact that when you start and run your own company, you benefit from its success. It's a great incentive to work hard.

The practice of law can be slow moving, and I was convinced that starting a company would be fast-paced, unpredictable, and even a lot of fun. Yet now that the project with Dominic wasn't moving forward, I needed to figure out my next step, and for a while I assumed that would involve working as a lawyer. Between my second and third years at Georgetown, I worked as a summer associate at a big New York law firm. At the end of the summer, the partners offered me a full-time job, and that's where I believed I was going after graduation the following spring. My plan was to work at the firm, make a little money, and then figure out how to get into business, maybe with Dominic.

It was a good plan, but it all changed the night I got back to Georgetown for the start of my final year of law school.

THAT NIGHT, I WENT OUT WITH A GROUP OF FRIENDS TO A bar called Dakota, in the Adams Morgan neighborhood in Northwest Washington. We happened to find ourselves near some fellow Georgetown law students, one of whom was a lovely young woman named April McClain, a second-year from Idaho. We chatted for a while, and later we danced, and I ended up giving her a lift home to her apartment. We didn't spend a lot of time together that evening—we were with a dozen or so friends, and the mood was casual—but I could tell there was something special about her.

The next day, I happened to see April in the lobby of the law school building. She was sitting at a table, looking through course descriptions and deciding which classes to take during the semester. I had already picked mine out, so I sat down and helped her with her selections. Given that I was a year ahead of her, I could reasonably behave as if I had some expertise in the matter. We ended up talking for a while, and eventually she went to the registrar's office to turn in her class selections. I waited about an hour and then went to the registrar's office myself. After dropping most of the classes I'd signed up for, I registered for the ones I'd just helped April select.

The following week, we struck up a conversation after one of those classes and I asked her out. We went to dinner, and for me that was all it took. April was not only smart, compelling, and beautiful, she was much more exposed to the world than I was: she had traveled extensively, and she spoke fluent Italian. I fell hard for her. Fortunately, she seemed to like me, too. In fact, her roommate at the time, Ilyse Schuman, would later joke that we went out on our first date and came back married—and that isn't too far from the truth. By Thanksgiving, April and I were already talking about getting married, and I proposed on her birthday the following May.

Meeting and marrying April is the greatest thing that has ever happened to me. For thirty years, she has been my partner in life and in public service. She is the heart and soul of our family, which now includes our four wonderful daughters. April's mom is from a large family in Logan, Utah, and her dad was a potato farmer from Idaho. April and her brother and sister were raised in Buhl, a small farm town not far from Twin Falls. Yet while their dad spent most of his days working on the family farm, he was also the chair of the Idaho Potato Farmers Association, which meant he traveled often to New York and Washington and sometimes brought his family along. These trips inspired April to think about a career in law and public policy.

A skilled regulatory lawyer, April did pioneering work in the international satellite services industry early in her career, and she now heads the Washington office of Common Sense Media. Founded by child advocate Jim Steyer in 2003, Common Sense is the country's leading nonprofit examining the effects of media and technology on children's health; April is not only the organization's Washington director, she also serves as a member of its national board.

Both April and I believe that the potential negative impact of media and technology on our children's well-being is one of the most pressing issues facing Americans today. The accelerating pace of technological innovation combined with the lack of desperately needed regulatory updates to the Communications Act of 1934 have created a challenging environment for kids, parents, and educators. Common Sense has a K–12 curriculum focused on cyber-bullying, privacy, tech addiction, and digital citizenship in more than one hundred thousands schools, and it recently partnered with a group of former technology executives to find new ways of protecting kids from digital manipulation and addiction. April and I have supported a variety of Common Sense's initiatives throughout the years, including funding a digital literacy campaign in the public schools of Montgomery County, Maryland.

April is also a nationally recognized advocate for children's media literacy and women's empowerment, and she serves on a number of nonprofit boards. Like me, she is dedicated to civility and bipartisanship, and she fulfills her many roles (lawyer, advocate, mother, wife, and friend to so many) with grace, intelligence, and strength. She has been the best possible partner in every aspect of my life, from parenthood to politics, and I'm so proud that she has been such a fine role model for our daughters. Back when we were in law school together, of course, this was all in the future, but it didn't take long for her to start changing my life in significant ways.

The summer after I graduated from law school, April and I lived with my parents in New Jersey while she worked at a respected law firm in New York City and I studied for the bar exam. In August, as she prepared to head back to Georgetown for her last year of law school, I got ready to start the job I'd been offered by the New York firm a year earlier. The notion of our being apart for the next ten months suddenly seemed unbearable. Though I passed the bar in both New York and New Jersey, I decided I'd rather be back in Washington with April. The only problem was I didn't have a job there.

I reached out to John Dealy, a law school professor at Georgetown I was close to. I knew that in addition to teaching he also worked at the well-known DC-based firm Shaw Pittman. He made some introductions at the firm, I had an interview a few days later, and on the Friday afternoon before Labor Day I received an offer. I hurried to call the New York firm to tell the partners I'd had a change of plans, but everyone had already left for the long weekend.

It didn't seem right to leave a voice mail message letting them know I was quitting, so on the Tuesday after Labor Day I showed up for my first, and last, day of work at the New York firm. I walked down the hall, passed an office with my newly engraved nameplate on the door, and went straight into the hiring partner's office to tell him I was no longer planning to work for the firm. The very next day, I started at Shaw Pittman in Washington, working on real estate matters in northern Virginia for a team of bright and talented partners.

My colleagues were terrific, and I liked the job very much. I learned a lot from the lawyers at the firm and still keep in touch with many of them. Even then, though, I knew it wouldn't be long before I ventured back into the world of entrepreneurship, because everything about it, from the freedom of being my own boss to the notion that if I worked hard enough the sky was the limit, felt irresistible to me. I just needed to find the right idea and the time to pursue it.

INCENTIVES ARE AN ESSENTIAL ELEMENT IN THE BUSINESS world. They're also a key part of civic life. When government introduces incentives into legislation, it can galvanize people to behave in ways that improve everyone's lives.

A perfect example of this is the estate tax. When a person dies, the U.S. government taxes the portion of the estate that exceeds a certain threshold, which the GOP's 2017 tax bill doubled from $11 million to $22 million. Because of the rule regarding estates, wealthy people will often make plans in advance to try to reduce that tax burden. One common way to do this is by donating to charities—which means the estate tax actually creates a massive incentive for people to give away their money.

Most Republicans favor repealing the estate tax altogether. Since Republicans are generally antitax, this isn't surprising, but the GOP rarely acknowledges how devastating such a move would be to the nonprofits that depend on charitable giving. I believe that the estate tax serves as an important way to prevent dynastic forms of wealth, which ultimately stifle the American dream.

What most people don't realize is that eliminating the estate tax also has the unintended consequence of slashing charitable giving.

The 1986 tax plan passed under President Reagan is another example of how government incentives have helped improve Americans' lives. For decades, people have cited this tax plan as convincing evidence that trickle-down economics works, but they're drawing the wrong lesson from the law's effect: trickle-down economics didn't work then and it doesn't work now.

When Reagan became president, the top marginal tax rate was very high, about 70 percent. But, in those days, the tax law also permitted lots of odd tax shelters, where you could invest your income in esoteric schemes as a way of avoiding paying taxes on it. For the most part, these shelters offered little or no economic return, but people didn't mind because they excluded significant income from taxes, which saved them from having to pay that 70 percent to the federal government.

That's bad economics. In a capitalistic system, you always want investment dollars flowing toward the highest return, but this money was just getting lost. What Reagan's tax plan did right was to cut taxes *and* get rid of the tax shelters. As a result, people started investing more efficiently, which in turn helped boost the economy.

For years, people have misunderstood the effect of the 1986 tax plan. They'll say, "Look, Reagan cut taxes, and the economy grew." The implication is that cutting taxes is a cure-all, but that is not at all the case. Reagan's plan (which was resoundingly bipartisan, passing the Senate by a vote of 74 to 23) worked because he changed the way people thought about deploying their marginal dollars. He changed the way they invested, and the returns benefited everyone. In the end, he worked with Republicans *and*

Democrats to reform the tax code in ways that were prescriptive to the issues of the time.

Today our nation is wrestling with a range of very difficult challenges. Among the issues we face are a lack of public-sector investment in infrastructure and basic research, an educational system that's contributing to a massive skills gap, an excessive concentration of wealth and opportunity, high levels of working poor, a lack of investment in huge swaths of our country, an accumulation of corporate profits overseas, and the growing threat of global climate change. Unfortunately, the Republican tax plan of 2017, which was approved on a party-line vote, failed to address almost all these complicated issues.

The GOP's fundamental failure was its inability to look beyond its own priorities. Good things happen when people behave in ways that benefit not only themselves but society as a whole. This is what we should focus on in government: How can we incentivize the population to behave in ways that help *all* Americans?

One way to do this is by expanding the earned income tax credit, or EITC. Before the EITC was established in the 1970s, there was a disincentive for some poor people to work as they could end up actually pocketing less money, because of taxes, than those who collected welfare. This was a terrible situation, as it essentially encouraged people to stay at home rather than get a job. The EITC changed that by giving a tax break to poor people who worked and earned money, thus giving them an incentive to continue working and earning more income.

The EITC is an excellent program. Every year, it helps keep millions of Americans from falling into poverty, and, like many successful programs, it has bipartisan support. Republicans like it because you have to work to get the tax break, so it's not a freebie. Democrats love it because it's an effective antipoverty program.

The main drawback to the EITC is that it doesn't reach enough Americans. We need to expand the program and increase both the number of people who are eligible and the amount of credit given. Right now, the EITC benefits primarily people who have children; we should broaden the eligibility rules to include childless workers, too, a simple fix that would have great impact. We should also expand the amount of the tax credit, thereby easing the path into the middle class. That's the kind of incentive that really motivates people to work: the promise that they'll be compensated for their labors in a way that makes getting and keeping a job truly worth their while.

For the 60 percent of American counties that have no economic upward mobility, a significant EITC expansion would provide a tremendous boost, lifting up the working poor in those hard-hit communities. Because of globalization and automation, the working class is likely to continue to struggle, while the investor class will in all likelihood continue to reap a disproportionate share of economic gains. But if we can ensure that people who work for a living earn the basic economic security needed to support their families and engage in society, we will drive pro-growth, "trickle-up" economics. That—and not the false promise of trickle-down economics—is the best way to ensure that the American dream remains broadly available.

FIGHTING CLIMATE CHANGE IS ANOTHER AREA WHERE WE can, and should, provide incentives for action. Climate change is *the* environmental challenge of our time, and if we don't act now to alter how human society behaves, it will be too late. While some politicians continue to argue over whether to believe the overwhelming scientific consensus on the matter, the private sector has wisely moved ahead. Standard and Poor's now includes resiliency to climate change in its modeling for sovereign credit ratings, and even oil companies such as ExxonMobil have built a price on carbon emissions into long-term business models.

Mark Carney, the governor of the Bank of England, has rightly argued that climate change poses a systemic risk to the global financial system. At some point, the financial markets may heed the warnings of Carney and others and begin to price the risk of climate change into carbon-intensive portfolios. If this were to happen too quickly, a dramatic change in the value of assets and the price of insurance risk could trigger another global financial meltdown.

While the business world is taking active measures, the U.S. government has completely abdicated its role as a leader in the effort to slow and ultimately reverse climate change. In 2017, the Trump administration shocked the world by rejecting the Paris climate agreement—the only country out of 197 to do so. This is bad not only for the environment but also for our economy. We should be positioning ourselves to be the leader in the new energy economy. Instead, we are the only nation in the world whose government refuses to acknowledge that climate change is occurring.

In 2014, I introduced legislation aimed at helping us achieve our environmental goals in the most effective market-based manner—by putting a price on carbon emissions. In addition to being the best way to reduce such emissions, carbon pricing would also produce revenue we could then use to help workers in the coal industry, aid low- and middle-income families, reduce taxes, and fund a massive expansion of the EITC.

Putting a price on carbon emissions is a free-market approach that would incentivize the private sector to innovate and thus provide a path into a clean energy economy. Currently, the incentives to reduce emissions are misaligned: the negative impact of the emissions falls on the world as a whole, rather than on the people creating those emissions. If we want to change behavior, we need to realign the incentives by making sure that the people who create the emissions are the ones paying for them.

If we use the revenues in the four ways I've described, we can make real progress in the battle against climate change while growing the economy *and* making sure that coal workers and low-income families don't face hardships because of reduced employment or higher energy costs. Even better, moving away from fossil fuels and toward sources of renewable energy will actually be a huge job creator, because fossil fuel jobs are highly mechanized while renewable energy jobs are far more labor-intensive.

GIVING PEOPLE AND COMPANIES INCENTIVES TO DO THE right thing is just one side of the coin. The other is removing the *disincentives* that stand in the way of success. Wherever there are roadblocks that keep Americans from achieving their greatest potential, we need to remove them.

One example of an inhibiting roadblock is health insurance. Too often, people in this country are afraid to leave their jobs because they're terrified of losing their health insurance. This has a particularly chilling effect on anyone who wants to become an entrepreneur or start a freelance career. If you're thinking about changing jobs, or simply leaving your job, the only question you should have to answer is whether it's a good move professionally—not whether you might end up broke or even bankrupt due to soaring health care costs or because you've experienced a medical crisis.

Americans have always been risk takers, and though we want people to be eager to take risks, we don't want them to risk their physical or financial health. As long as health care is linked to employment, though, there will be a real lack of mobility in the workforce—and that hurts workers, companies, and ultimately the entire American economy.

The solution to this problem is clear: we need to create a public option, one that would be essentially a nonprofit health insurance company chartered by the federal government. This "company" would participate in the individual health care exchanges, thereby ensuring competition in each market. The public option could even use the existing Medicare provider network as a launching pad for its services. And according to the experts at the Congressional Budget Office, adding a public option would also have the side benefit of decreasing the deficit.

After fixing the ACA, we could then begin the work of designing a system that enshrines the principle that health care is the right of every American. The most successful part of the ACA was the expansion of Medicaid; unfortunately, some states chose not to expand, and some individuals chose not to buy insurance on the exchanges. My plan would give every American citizen under the age of Medicare eligibility the option to receive free Medicaid-type health care. These plans could be structured in a variety of ways depending upon people's income and needs.

Anyone who wants such a plan could have it. And unlike those who argue for a single-payer system, I wouldn't *force* all Americans to participate in a government health care plan. Those who didn't want the government plan could instead choose to accept credit toward buying a private insurance plan, or perhaps buy a supplemental plan. This way, the choice would remain with the American people. Best of all, everyone would be covered, regardless of his or her employment status or situation.

The way to pay for this system is through incentives. We must allow the government to negotiate with pharmaceutical companies on drug prices, eliminate the health care tax deduction for employers, and recognize the cost to the system of the uncompensated care already occurring in emergency rooms. It makes no sense for the largest customer in the United States, the federal government, not to be able to negotiate volume discounts on health care pricing. Reliable estimates show that this one change would save us $110 billion over ten years. Also, once health insurance expenses are no longer tax deductible, employers will probably stop offering health care plans directly. This would provide two benefits: companies would be better able to boost wages (which *are* deductible) and individuals would be more aware of the true cost of health care. Far too much money is wasted in the health care system by consumers who don't feel any linkage between behavior and costs. (For example, obesity is estimated to cost us $147 billion in health care annually.) People who are aware of the actual cost of their health care are more likely to change their diet and behavior in ways that will help lower those costs.

Essentially, we would shift the burden of health care costs so that employers could spend more time focusing on what they *should* be focusing on, which is the nuts and bolts of running their companies and making them more successful. At the same time, we would be ensuring that every American had access to health insurance—either free insurance from the government or, if they preferred, a private plan that they partially paid for. Nothing would prevent employers from arranging and managing health care plans for their employees—and I suspect most would do so— or from creating pools to share risk among employees to help get better deals. Still, eliminating health care tax deductions would essentially decouple health insurance from one's place of employment, currently many people's only path to health care.

In summary, this new system would:

- free employees to make employment decisions based on what they *should* be made on—that is, whether changing or leaving a job is a good career move;

- free employers from the business of managing the unpredictability of health care costs, which has clearly had a major effect on historical wage growth;

- bring consumers closer to their own health care costs, which will prove to be an effective tool for controlling costs over time;

- maintain an incentive for the private economy to invest in health care (today, both Medicaid and Medicare pay providers only 80–95 percent of their costs, while private insurers pay 110–120 percent of their costs. One big issue with single-payer plans is, Will the government cover the cost? And if not, what happens to quality?);

- encourage the creation of free public health clinics for Medicaid beneficiaries, where doctors are employees and not fee-for-service providers, and where patient-provider relationships are created that can incentivize preventative care;

- allow us to holistically address mental health care, focusing on the scale of the mental health crisis and better understanding the impact that poverty, violence, social media, and economic stress all have on Americans' mental health.

Unlike a single-payer plan, the system I'm proposing would be affordable to taxpayers. It would also address the real health care issues we're facing, but it would do so without eliminating the existing plans that so many people like. Most important, it would make health care a right for every American.

THE QUOTE THAT OPENS THIS CHAPTER IS FROM CHARLIE Munger, a well-known investor and Warren Buffett's partner in Berkshire Hathaway. A brilliant thinker in investing philosophy, Munger offers advice that's as straightforward as it is insightful. "Never, ever, think about something else when you should be thinking about the power of incentives," he has written. I tend to agree with him, though of course it's important to focus on the right kind of incentives.

I'm a big believer in capitalism, but I'd like to see a world where capitalism became more just, more inclusive; where companies paid better, embraced equality and family-friendly practices, improved benefits, invested in their communities, and promoted environmental stewardship. Part of that is about changing the incentives and creating more transparency.

In the financial services industry, which is where I built my business career, it's common to compensate employees based on pure financial metrics. Yet that approach seemed narrow and potentially damaging to me. Employees get pretty good at figuring out how to meet formulas or quotas, with the expectation that they'll be rewarded, but they're not incentivized to care about their colleagues, or focus on their workplace culture, or ask larger questions about risk and reward and where their company and their industry might be heading. The truth is that incentives around compensation can lead to bad behavior that hurts some stakeholders, so at my companies we avoided those types of incentives.

We also provided significant equity ownership to employees, which not only served to align their interests with those of the company but addressed a shortcoming of our system of capitalism. Since entering Congress, I've advanced legislation in this area, in an attempt to ensure that workers have equity in the U.S. economy. We also promoted transparency and talked openly about our commitment to our community. With the help of organizations such as JUST Capital, which ranks companies based on their commitment to addressing the issues American people care about, we're beginning to see a welcome accountability in the private sector.

We want people to live up to their highest ideals, but human nature is such that many of us don't always listen to our better angels. This has been true throughout history, and it's particularly relevant to our political situation today.

One of the biggest problems with our current political system is that people are incentivized to be partisan. Gerrymandering, which has spread like wildfire over the past few decades, has encouraged politicians to be hyperpartisan and has contributed to a situation in which 80 percent of congressional districts are "safe" for the party that holds them. As a result, the elected officials in those districts have no incentive to listen to the half of our country that holds different political views. Increasingly, the loudest, most radical voices on either side of the aisle have the greatest likelihood of being heard, and the vast majority of people in the middle is, in too many cases, ignored.

The result is a country that's deeply divided, with each side failing, and often refusing, to communicate with the other. We've got to change the way people are incentivized to participate in our nation's politics, stop rewarding division and hyperpartisanship, and encourage a system where communication, collaboration, and bipartisanship are rewarded.

CHAPTER 5

Think Different

Creativity is seeing what everyone else has seen, and
thinking what no one else has thought.

ALBERT EINSTEIN

WHILE I WAS IN LAW SCHOOL, I GOT TO KNOW A FELLOW
student named Ethan Leder. He was a year ahead of me, and
though I could see right away that he was smart and a lot of fun
to be around, we became good friends in part because, like me,
he also wanted to be an entrepreneur. Ethan and I started one
business together, a newsletter company, before I even left law
school, but it didn't go anywhere. Still, he and I kept tossing
around ideas, looking for the right opportunity to come along.

About a year after my graduation, while I was working at the
firm in DC and Ethan was at a firm in Baltimore, we stumbled
across a classified ad in the *Washington Post* that seemed promising.
A very small home health care company, part of a larger franchised

operation, was for sale for just fifteen thousand dollars. The company had six employees, and it was struggling financially, but Ethan and I didn't care because the price was right.

In some ways, it made sense for us to be drawn to a health care company. I had majored in biology, had seriously considered becoming a doctor, and had worked in hospitals. And, of course, I could always ask Uncle Jack for advice and expertise if I needed it. For Ethan's part, his dad, who chairs the Department of Genetics at Harvard, is arguably one of the most influential geneticists of our time. Yet those weren't the reasons we bought the company. The truth is we wanted to find out if we could run a business, and this was just about the only one we could afford.

We scraped together the money and bought the company, and after exactly one year of practicing law, I left my big, comfortable firm and went full-time into the health care business. Ethan and I were pretty confident that we could continue delivering the company's basic service, which was to provide nurses for home care in the Washington, DC, metropolitan area, serving mostly Medicaid and Medicare patients. We'd have to learn everything else on the fly, from managing people to recruiting to billing and accounting.

Ethan and I dove in, trying to learn as much as we could in as short a time as possible. We soon realized we were screwed. Our little company, which we renamed Leddel Health, based on a combination of our last names, was the worst home care agency in the city. We were truly the call of last resort; people turned to us when they couldn't get anyone else to come.

Many months later, we barely had enough patients to make payroll. Most were discharges from DC General Hospital and Greater Southeast Hospital, so we went to these hospitals and spoke to the discharge planners, practically begging them to give us more business. They would tell us, "Well, we have all these other companies we normally use, so why should we change?" We couldn't get any traction, so for the first year the business limped along, barely solvent.

Finally, we got a break. We became one of the first home care companies to switch its business model to "capitation," charging a flat monthly fee rather than a per-patient fee. By streamlining in this way, we managed to persuade Kaiser Permanente to give us a contract for $35,000 a month to provide its home care in the area. This was a huge boost; it stabilized the business and allowed us to hire more people. Still, by that time, Ethan and I had learned enough about home health care to realize there was a better business opportunity than the one we'd been pursuing. It was related to an emerging industry called home infusion therapy.

This was the early 1990s, a time when intravenous medicines were increasingly being delivered in the home, mostly for patients suffering from HIV/AIDS or cancer. These patients needed nurses to come to their houses, connect their IVs, and then come back four hours later and carefully remove them. Companies had sprung up specifically to fill this need—they were sort of mobile pharmacies, and they hired the nurses in health care companies such as ours to do the actual work.

These home infusion companies were profitable because they saved the health insurance companies the much higher cost of having all those patients check into hospitals for treatment. So instead of simply providing our nurses for a fee, Ethan and I pivoted and started our own home infusion company, which we named American Home Therapies. We partnered with a woman who was seasoned in the industry, Marianne Lowry, to run the operation, and the business took off rapidly. Too rapidly, in fact.

Soon we were successful enough that we had a hard time funding the company's growth. And that was how we discovered yet another niche in the health care market that needed filling.

Insurance companies usually took three to four months to pay us, but every week we had to pay our nurses' salaries and our pharmacy bills. This gap in working capital was hard to bridge, and because we had no track record, we couldn't get any banks to lend us money. We desperately needed financing, but where could we get it? After months of frustrated searching, we finally found a company in Dallas that specialized in lending money to small health care companies.

Like us, the guy who founded that company, Richard Metcalfe, was a lawyer turned entrepreneur, so we got along well right from the start. With the advances his company provided, we were able to even out our cash flow and continue to grow the business. Just a few years after starting American Home Therapies, Ethan and I were able to sell it for a nice profit. Now we were officially entrepreneurs.

As good as our business had become, we realized that Richard Metcalfe had an even better one. Small to midsize health care companies had a real need for financing, and very few financial institutions were willing to fill that need. So Ethan and I, along with another good friend and law school classmate, Ed Nordberg, pivoted again. In 1993 we decided to start our own health care financing company.

I had just turned thirty, and April and I had a new baby, Summer, the first of our four daughters. With three years of entrepreneurial experience now under my belt, I was energized by our success and excited about this new venture. We flew to Dallas to ask Richard to help us start the business and mentor us, and in return we offered him a percentage of the company. He told us he was game. He'd already been shrinking his business and edging toward retirement, so he was happy to help us get into the industry.

We set up shop, named our fledgling firm HealthPartners Financial Corporation (later changed to HealthCare Financial Partners), and raised initial capital from the Tennessee-based investor group Gerber/Taylor. It soon became clear that our instincts were dead-on: almost from the first day, the business took off.

Within a year, we needed another infusion of capital to further grow the company. That's when a friend and shareholder introduced me to a couple of investors in San Francisco, Jason Fish and Tom Steyer. A few years earlier, Tom had founded the Farallon Capital Management hedge fund, and he was widely regarded as a smart investor. In time, Farallon would become one of the most successful private investment firms in the country, and Tom would later become a good friend and well-known Democratic activist. (He's the guy who, in the fall of 2017, famously bought billboards in Times Square urging the impeachment of President Trump.)

Farallon invested $25 million, with Jason Fish managing the investment. This propelled us into the big leagues: within three years, we were successful enough to take the company public. On the day of our initial public offering, in September 1996, Health-Care Financial Partners was worth $86 million. We initially listed the company on the NASDAQ, and then, a year later, on the New York Stock Exchange, where, one morning in December 1997, I became the youngest CEO of a company on the NYSE.

That was when I went to ring the opening bell at the stock exchange, looked across the Hudson River, and remembered all those thank-you speeches I'd given to the electricians at the IBEW local in Jersey City. Back then, I could never have dreamed that

I'd achieve so much as an entrepreneur, but there was better yet to come. We kept on growing the business, hiring people, and financing hundreds of health care companies. In 1999, we sold our company to Heller Financial for $500 million.

IN THE DAYS WHEN ETHAN, ED, AND I WERE BUILDING OUR businesses, I spent a lot of time thinking about business principles and what made companies successful. In the case of Health-Care Financial Partners, we succeeded because we were good at coming up with creative solutions to other companies' financing needs and because we moved quickly and got things done fast. Often, companies like those we dealt with would be growing like crazy but unable to find a traditional bank that would lend to them, so we brought in a lot of business by being flexible and coming up with innovative ways to make loans happen.

As I saw it, our job was to support these fledgling companies, taking care to do so in ways that were prudent for us as a lender. To that end, we focused on the "original path to yes." This meant that if someone came in and asked for a loan, and the people making the pitch seemed honest and ethical, and the risk-adjusted return attractive, the answer would be yes. Then we'd have to find an original way of getting it done—because if the usual way were an option, a traditional bank would already have provided the necessary funds. To make these loans, we knew we'd have to think outside the box, either by managing credit risk in a unique manner or by executing the transaction faster than anyone else.

"Think different" is best known as an Apple marketing slogan, but it can be applied to any kind of business, not to mention nonprofits and the government. It's surprising how often the answer to a difficult and pervasive problem can be found in a simple, creative solution.

Take the example of Muhammad Yunus. Born in 1940 in a small Bengali village, one of fourteen children, Yunus grew up seeing the ravages of poverty all around him. Smart and ambitious, he excelled in school and ultimately became an economist and professor. At age thirty-four, he had an experience that changed not only his life but eventually the lives of millions of people—first on the Indian subcontinent and then all over the world.

He had taken a group of students to a small village where they interviewed a woman who was making and selling bamboo stools. The woman explained that in order to buy raw bamboo, she had to borrow small sums of money, but the only lenders who would provide the funds charged exorbitant rates, up to 10 percent *per week*. This was devastating to her tiny business: because of the high cost of borrowing, the woman was able to clear only about a penny per stool.

Professor Yunus was dismayed by the woman's story. She was trying to earn an honest living, but because she had nothing to offer as collateral, no traditional bank in the world would lend her money. Her only choice was to turn to these alternative lenders, but their high rates meant that she'd never be able to do anything more than keep her head above water. Yunus couldn't bear to think of her working so hard while having so little hope of improving her situation, especially as the amount of money she needed to fund her business was so small.

In the end, he decided to lend her the money himself. In fact, he offered to lend money to three dozen such women in the village—a grand total of about twenty-seven dollars. Yet even that tiny amount would be enough to give these women a realistic chance of creating sustainable small businesses, anything from selling fruit, to providing sewing services, to making pottery.

Yunus's original "micro-loan" to the woman making bamboo stools proved to be the seed of a groundbreaking idea. In 1983, he founded Grameen Bank, a nonprofit organization that lent small sums of money to poor women (initially in Bangladesh) seeking to escape the cycle of poverty. Grameen, which means "of the village" in Bengali, was built on the novel premise that groups of borrowers would be responsible for one another. If any member defaulted on her loan, everyone else in the group lost their loans, too. This was Yunus's innovative solution to the problem of lending to people with no collateral: the women didn't want to let down the others in their group, so nearly everyone made her payments on time. In fact, the rate of repayment for Grameen's loans stands at an astounding 97 percent.

In the thirty-five years since Grameen's founding, numerous organizations and even some for-profit companies have followed in its footsteps. Micro-lending has grown into a multibillion-dollar industry, serving families all over the world, including in poverty-stricken parts of the United States. In 2006, Yunus and Grameen were jointly awarded the Nobel Peace Prize.

The story of Grameen shows how a deeply complex problem can be solved by a simple idea. By thinking differently about the problem of poverty, Muhammad Yunus improved millions of people's lives. The challenge for us is how to apply that kind of out-of-the-box thinking to government.

As someone with experience in both business and politics, I love the Grameen story because it combines progressive ideas with market-based solutions. Many people tend to think of these two things as opposing forces, but a lot of good can come out of finding ways to combine them.

For those on the left, the private economy is often seen as having values that are questionable at best, immoral at worst. The "free market" often evokes notions of unchecked greed and ambition. Yet while there are indeed people and companies that fit that profile, there are bad actors in every walk of life. In my experience, the overwhelming majority of participants in the private sector are good people. To condemn the entire private economy as a greed machine feeding the 1 percent is to miss the point entirely. In fact, our ever changing, remarkably dynamic economy has helped make the United States an exceptionally strong, upwardly mobile, innovative nation. Besides, how can you be pro-jobs and antibusiness when the private economy employs the vast majority of workers in this country?

My policies are often progressive, but I'm also a businessman. To my mind, the way to advance our ideals is not by fighting against the private economy but by working with it. In purely pragmatic terms, doing so will make us stronger both financially and politically.

For those who suggest that the Democratic Party should move farther left and embrace socialism, I would argue that there's no credible evidence that this evolution would win us more elections or gain more support. There are also no persuasive data suggesting that any other nation has a better economic model than ours. Using the wedge of the private economy to split our party into two opposing factions is the last thing we should do, because now more than ever we need to be unified. And the way to bring the Democratic Party together is by thinking

beyond the traditional, restrictive ideas about how party and ideology are structured.

One of the biggest problems with any ideological approach is
that some people hold firm, uncompromising opinions on just
about every issue that's ever been debated in politics. There's no
room for discussion, creativity, or nuance; these people will give
you their answer before you even finish posing the question. Ask
a dyed-in-the-wool Republican about raising taxes, and the answer
will be an automatic "no." Ask most true-blue Democrats about
education reform, and the answer will be an automatic "no."

If, in 1983, you had asked any banker in the world, "Would
you consider handing out millions in loans to poor people who
have no collateral?" the answer would also have been an automatic
"no." Yet Muhammad Yunus resisted that knee-jerk impulse and
dreamed up a different way to lend, and in doing so he changed
the world. I wouldn't presume to compare HealthCare Financial
Partners to Grameen, but I suspect that most American busi-
nesspeople probably wouldn't have thought that three young entrepreneurs with no experience in finance could lend money to
hundreds of health care companies shunned by the banks and have
no losses on any of their loans. Yet that's what Ethan, Ed, and I
were able to do with our company.

Here's a question all politicians should ask themselves: How
many creative governing solutions are we missing because we're
afraid of stepping outside our ideological boxes? We need to push
past the natural human tendency to become rooted in one side,
and we need to learn to approach problem solving in a more pragmatic way, less like ideologues and more like entrepreneurs.

Being a good entrepreneur requires qualities such as creativity, passion, tenacity, and flexibility. The American marketplace

is relentlessly competitive, and you must be able to innovate and to pivot when necessary. You have to be good at selling your ideas, getting buy-in, and building consensus. Perhaps most important, you must be relentlessly honest about the facts of your situation. These traits hold the key to your becoming a successful entrepreneur, but aren't these also traits you would like to see in your elected officials, from the president on down?

Let's take the analogy further. One of the lessons the business world teaches is that you *sell* to your clients, but you're *responsible* to your shareholders, who look to you for leadership, a steady hand, honesty, and returns on their investment. Back when I first ran for public office, I started thinking about how this model might apply in government.

When you're the president of the United States, trying to advance your domestic policy, Congress is your client; you should be relentlessly selling your agenda to Congress and developing personal relationships with each member. Your path to accomplishing anything in domestic policy runs through Congress, so they're the people you must persuade to buy in to whatever you're proposing. And while it's true that the president can achieve certain goals through executive action, the really transformative things (building infrastructure, solving the student debt crisis, overhauling the health care system) all depend on getting that buy-in. There is no more important use of your time, and you have to check your ego at the door to get it done.

The American people are your shareholders. They have entrusted their investment to you, and they're depending on you to achieve certain gains or progress for them. With every vote I cast and every bill I support, I'm always thinking about what kind of return it will bring to the people who've placed their trust in me. Sometimes I think back to that Social Security workshop in Gaithersburg, Maryland, and remember how even at a moment of extreme partisan anger, people applauded the notion that I was deeply committed to bipartisanship. In my experience, people care a lot less about partisan ideology than they do about real progress.

This is the way to move forward—with a focus on pragmatic solutions that incorporate the best that both sides have to offer. My infrastructure bill, with its mix of business incentives and public improvements, follows this strategy. So does my proposal for closing the skills gap through national service and apprenticeships, which benefits both the private and the public sectors. Once you cast aside partisan differences and commit to making things happen, the possibilities for progress are endless.

HERE'S ONE MORE EXAMPLE OF LEGISLATION THAT TAKES the best of both sides and comes up with a creative solution: the Investing in Opportunity Act, a bill I cosponsored.

First, a little background. The organizing economic principle of the past couple of decades has been globalization. In some ways, humanity has been sorted based on globalization's winners and losers—meaning that over the last several decades, your village or city or county has seen increased or decreased capital flow. On the whole, the United States is doing fine. Many of the expected benefits of globalization have been realized: our standard of living has improved, we have benefited from lower prices and more choices, and foreign export markets have opened. At the local level, though, many American communities have been devastated. In addition, while globalization has rewarded people who have excellent educations or highly specialized skills, it has punished people from the old-line manufacturing economy.

The new wave of globalization has made it possible for companies to move their production overseas. This has been great for many big corporations' bottom lines, but it has also led to plants closing, workers being laid off, jobs being outsourced, and capital drying up in towns across America. At the same time, we've seen spectacular growth in industries such as information technology, biotechnology, and energy. Thousands of businesses in the service industries have benefited, and countless numbers of investors and entrepreneurs have built companies and created jobs. But although we've had plenty of capital investment on a net basis, it has rarely gone to the communities that lost it; instead, most of it has gone to our largest cities, primarily on the coasts. Fully 80 percent of professionally managed venture capital flows into New York, Boston, and northern California, and although all that money is creating jobs, raising home values, and driving up wages, the vast majority of the communities in our country is being left behind.

America's economy is remarkably resilient, and I'm confident that it will continue to grow. But it won't truly thrive until we figure out a way to get capital flowing back into the places that have lost it. How can we accomplish this?

There are two types of capital, public and private. If we want to move public capital into these distressed communities, we can do it through infrastructure. We can build things, which has the additional advantages of creating jobs and, ultimately, an environment that will attract private capital. If you live in a rural community and don't have broadband Internet, for instance, no private business is going to set up shop in your town. But if the government comes in and builds out the broadband network, businesses are much more likely to give your community a closer look. This is the strategy underlying my infrastructure bill.

Yet maybe there's another way to attract private capital to places that have been left behind by economic change. How else can we persuade people to invest in these areas, as opposed to the big coastal cities? The solution lies, not surprisingly, in a pragmatic combination of business and public incentives.

As I write this, Americans are sitting on about $3 trillion in appreciated stocks and other assets. If they sell these assets, they'll be required to pay capital gains taxes on what they've made—and because most of us loathe paying taxes, many of us sit on appreciated stocks rather than selling them. The Investing in Opportunity Act incentivizes people to cash out those assets and put them to work. Here's the idea at the heart of this bill.

Let's say that a few years ago you bought Amazon stock at $100 a share, and now it's up to $1,100. Under current laws, if you sell that stock, you have to pay capital gains taxes on your $1,000-a-share profit, no matter what. What the Investing in Opportunity Act proposes is that, instead, you can take that profit and invest it in an "opportunity zone," meaning a community in a part of the country that has been identified as lagging economically. If you choose to invest in rebuilding that community, you can defer paying your capital gains tax for ten years.

Not everyone will be eager to invest their capital gains in this way, and that's fine. But I'm convinced that a significant number of people, because they either hate taxes or see opportunity in these investments, will want to take advantage of this option. This means that instead of having all that capital locked up in unsold assets, we could liberate tens of billions of dollars of capital to flow directly into the communities that need it most. It's a win-win solution.

As a general rule, Republicans approve of any method that saves people from paying taxes, while Democrats like creating incentives for private money to flow to communities that need it. And even though many Republicans typically resist these types of tax incentives, there's still enough support from the GOP to make this bill, like the infrastructure bill, truly bipartisan.

The Investing in Opportunity Act addresses a complex problem in a simple and creative way. Although there were many things wrong with the 2017 Republican tax bill—the worst being that it will explode our deficit just to give tax cuts to wealthy individuals, who absolutely don't need them—I was delighted when the Investing in Opportunity Act was added into the final version of the bill. For all the talk of how politicians have no interest whatsoever in bipartisanship, anytime you see people from opposite sides of the aisle combining forces, it's hard not to conclude that whatever they're supporting is worthwhile. We are stronger when we identify a common goal and then work together to achieve it.

THERE'S ANOTHER ISSUE THAT TENDS TO CAUSE KNEE-JERK responses from both Democrats and Republicans: deficits. Both parties argue that their policies are fiscally responsible. After all, who would ever argue the opposite? But despite the fact that, in 2017, Republicans checked their fiscal responsibility at the door when they approved a tax bill that's projected to grow the deficit by over $1 trillion, the GOP has historically tended to believe that our country should have annual deficits of zero. On the other side of the aisle, Democrats tend to believe that the size of our annual deficits don't necessarily matter. In my view, both these positions are flawed. Here's why.

The Republican position is that if hardworking American families don't spend more than they take in, why should their government? This thinking is flawed for two reasons. First, American families sometimes do spend more than they take in, such as when they get mortgages to buy houses or take out loans to pay for their kids to go to college. It's not wrong or even dangerous for people to carry debt, as long as that debt doesn't get out of control and they're investing in an asset with real value. Second, if we tried to run the government without relying on debt, we would be massively underinvesting in our country for no good reason. Spending encourages economic growth, which is the key to creating a better future for everyone. Just as families must manage their mortgages and credit card debt, so the government needs to make sure that, over the long term, our deficits don't exceed our rate of economic growth.

Some Democrats err in the opposite direction. They argue that deficits don't matter, and as a result, they propose major programs while giving little thought to the question of how to pay for them. The problem with our current level of debt as a percentage of our total economy is that when interest rates go up, as they almost certainly will, the interest on our debt will crowd out everything we care about. We're fortunate to be living in a period when interest rates have been extremely low for a sustained stretch of time. But if you look at historical averages, interest rates should be about three times as high as they are now. Currently, the interest we pay on our deficit as a percentage of our budget is about 7 percent; if that percentage were to soar to, say, 20 percent, it would cause a tremendous problem. By not addressing our national debt in a prudent, long-term manner, we are leaving our children a heavy and, arguably, immoral burden.

What is an acceptable level for the deficit? People talk a lot about how big our national debt is; at the end of 2017, it stood at around $20 trillion. But that's not actually the number that matters. What matters is this number: the deficit as a percentage of our economy. Historically, the United States has managed debt as a percentage of the economy at 50 percent to 55 percent. Today, it's over 75 percent, and with the passage of the GOP tax bill, it's now expected to grow to nearly 100 percent in the next ten years. That level of debt isn't just scary; it is unsustainable.

The ideal solution is to manage our economy so that deficits remain at rates that are slightly lower than the annual growth of our GDP—which, in 2018, would mean targeting the deficit at about 2.0 percent, since the economy should be able to grow at over 2.5 percent. Finding a way to hit that target would be great for the American economy, because it would mean that, on average, our debt, as a percentage of the economy, would go down a bit every year.

Sounds pretty sensible, doesn't it? The problem is we can't hit a target until we come up with one, and these days, our elected officials can't agree on a fiscally responsible target because we can't even agree on a common goal. But if we could get lawmakers to come out of their respective corners and meet in this middle ground to agree on a goal based on simple economics, it would completely change the debate in Congress. We just have to be willing to think a little differently about the problem and then agree to join forces to work toward a mutual solution.

....

CHAPTER 6

Release America's Inner Entrepreneur

To succeed, jump as quickly at opportunities as you do at conclusions.

BENJAMIN FRANKLIN

AFTER SELLING HEALTHCARE FINANCIAL PARTNERS IN 1999, I decided to take time away from business and focus on spending quality time with my family. The kids were growing up, and I wanted to be an active and involved dad in their formative years; Summer, our eldest, was seven, Brooke was three, and our third daughter, Lily, was on the way. We as a family also wanted to explore how we could take some of the profits made from the sale of the company to do good in the community and give back some of the blessings we had received.

We funded the Delaney Family Fund through the Community Foundation of the National Capital Region as a means of getting more deeply involved in philanthropy. I also got very involved with Summer's school, St. Patrick's Episcopal Day School, and joined the boards of Georgetown University, the National Symphony Orchestra, the Potomac School, and the Boys and Girls Club of Greater Washington.

April would later join a number of boards, including those of the Northwestern School of Communication; the foundation board of the Children's National Medical Center; the International Center for Research on Women; the Georgetown Institute for Women, Peace, and Security; Common Sense Media; and the Community School in Idaho. She would also go on to chair the Georgetown University Law Center board.

We focused our efforts in a few key areas, including funding educational projects at a variety of institutions and levels, spanning from preschool to graduate school; educational efforts at Common Sense Media (including how media impact the health and well-being of children); and efforts to empower women around the globe socially, economically, and politically. We also supported efforts aimed at providing core services for the poor through Catholic Charities and worked with excellent organizations active in economically challenged communities, such as Vision to Learn and the Baltimore-based Center for Urban Families.

The thrust of our efforts over the past ten years, however, has been on advocating issues related to girls. April and I have four daughters, and we both believe strongly that when women have equal support and participation in every sphere of society, from politics to business to family life, everyone benefits. To that end, in 2014, we endowed the Hillary Clinton Fellowship at the Georgetown Institute for Women, Peace, and Security, headed by our good friend Ambassador Melanne Verveer.

We were happy to be spreading our wings and eager to make

a difference where we could, so giving back was, and will continue to be, a big part of our family ethos. But after some time at home, I still felt the tug of the entrepreneurial world. And having just come off a successful run as CEO and founder of a company, I was also being offered a lot of opportunities to run start-ups.

This was 1999, the height of the first dot-com boom, but although several high-profile Internet start-ups were pursuing me as CEO, none of them felt like the right fit. Unlike many of today's high-flying technology companies, which have truly disruptive business models and are fundamentally changing commerce, many companies during the late 1990s boom felt like little more than a name with ".com" attached; they had no real business model but very high valuations.

Maybe I was old-fashioned (though I was still only in my midthirties), but when I did a deep dive into the business models for these shiny new companies, they just didn't make sense to me. Looking closely at the expected sustainability of the businesses and their ability to predictably generate cash flow, I didn't find much of substance there. Mostly they seemed to be betting on the "greater fool theory"—that is, buying something with no intrinsic value on the theory that someone would pay more for it in the future. This was a gamble I had no interest in making. After a year of considering various offers, I set my sights on starting another company focused on what I loved, which was lending money to small and midsize companies and helping great entrepreneurs achieve their dreams.

After six years of growing a health care lending company, I realized that many elements of that business were applicable to other industries as well. I also sensed a unique opportunity in the credit cycle. As far as I could tell, big banks were becoming focused on two sectors: lending to very large companies, with whom they could also do investment banking; and consumer lending, meaning mortgages and credit cards. Yet the banks had pretty much stopped lending to midsize companies. We had successfully filled that niche for health care, so why not broaden our approach and work with similar-size companies in other industries, such as retail, software, and security?

I went back to Tom Steyer and Jason Fish of Farallon and pitched them on this new idea. Both of them saw the potential, and Jason, who by this point had become a good friend, decided to join the enterprise as my partner. We named the company CapitalSource, and Farallon almost immediately committed to investing $200 million. Before the year was out we had several other investors, including a well-respected firm named Madison Dearborn, where I had gotten to know a partner named Tim Hurd. We also developed a great relationship with a top lender at a major bank, Jim Sigman at First Union. Before we even opened our doors in 2000, First Union had agreed to lend us $250 million based on my track record at HealthCare Financial. We would go on to raise a total initial investment of half a billion dollars; at the time, this made us the largest-funded start-up in history.

CapitalSource's core business was making loans to fast-growing small- to middle-market companies. We wanted to help them grow by financing important events or opportunities for those companies. Our business plan was simple: instead of relying on generalists to decide which companies to loan money to, we organized teams of specialists by industry. We were also committed to providing great service.

As a member of the credit committee, I was deeply involved in assessing the loans. I met many of the loan-seeking management teams personally, and I approved every loan we gave out—in just over a decade, more than $20 billion to upwards of four thousand companies. One of my favorite tasks was listening to people lay out their business plans; I was fascinated by the many kinds of businesses these entrepreneurs were growing. In fact, this job gave me a singular window into the U.S. economy and a deep understanding not only of how it really works but also of the kinds of companies that are actually creating jobs.

Small businesses are great, and about half of the private-sector workers in this country are employed by them, but think about your local deli or dry cleaner—even if it's a successful business, it's not likely to expand rapidly and hire dozens of new employees. At the other end of the scale, big companies don't tend to create a lot of new jobs, either; more often, they grow by buying other companies and then laying people off. The fact is the vast majority of net new jobs created in this country comes from the "gazelles," midsize companies that experience hockey stick growth, shooting up from, say, five employees to a thousand.

When we started CapitalSource, these types of companies were growing too fast for most community banks, but they still weren't big enough to be targeted by the big banks. Our timing, therefore, was perfect. We had found a niche that needed filling, and with our half billion dollars in equity capital, we were able to jump right in and start lending. CapitalSource took off pretty much immediately.

We made sure to take care of our employees, figuring that offering the best benefits and a family-friendly work environment would make us a magnet for talent—which it did. We paid well, and we offered generous benefits, including health care, a 401(k) match, and paid family leave. We had a gym installed in the office for everyone to use, brought in nurses to give flu shots to anyone who wanted one, and were one of the first companies to provide everyone with an amazing new device called a BlackBerry. Unusually for a financial services company, we even offered free lunch for everyone. We figured the cost per person would be only about six dollars per lunch—an easy investment to make, because it meant our team members would be able to get home a half hour earlier each day. For a company with a lot of young families, that perk was like gold.

We also hired differently. Based in the DC area, we could draw from a large pool of talented lawyers, and they became a big part of our workforce. I particularly like hiring lawyers. They are detail-oriented and tend to focus on the downside as much as on the upside. And because our lawyers were able to take in large volumes of information quickly and surmise where the problems in a given business lay, CapitalSource soon developed a reputation for performing our due diligence quickly.

Just three years after founding CapitalSource, Jason and I took it public, and before turning forty I became the CEO of my second NYSE company. In those three years, the start-up Jason and I founded had grown to the point where we employed approximately 250 people and had made $2.9 billion in loans to small to midsize businesses all over the United States. Our initial public offering raised an additional $300 million in equity capital to fund our growth; the way I saw it, we were just getting started. I was proud of these accomplishments but, as the years passed, I was even prouder that CapitalSource was regularly named one of the most admired companies in the Washington, DC, area. In 2010, the Obama administration gave us the Bank Enterprise Award for lending money in an ethical manner to disadvantaged communities.

For eighteen years (from 1993 until 2011, when I resigned as CEO to run for Congress), I was fortunate enough to spend my days listening to entrepreneurs talk about their ideas and figuring out how to finance the development of fast-growing businesses. This experience not only taught me a great deal about how the private economy works in this country but also showed how much entrepreneurs can do to change things for the better. We had the privilege of financing the success of thousands of companies in forty-five states, and, in turn, these companies created hundreds of thousands of jobs. My work at both HealthCare Financial and CapitalSource informs my work as a member of Congress to this day. A lot of politicians talk about "jobs, jobs, jobs," but I'm one of the few who has actually created thousands of them, while also helping thousands of companies collectively create hundreds of thousands more.

IF YOU SPEND TIME TALKING TO PEOPLE IN BUSINESS, academia, or the nonprofit sector, you see the world from a very different perspective than those who have spent their whole lives inside the political bubble. Too often, politics consists of relitigating the past rather than focusing on the future. As a businessman who came to politics later in life—I was forty-eight when I decided to run for office for the first time—I'm eager to turn our political focus to the future of our nation and the larger world we live in. And in my view that means that if the United States is going to continue to thrive, we have to learn to be more entrepreneurial.

Thinking and acting like an entrepreneur doesn't come naturally to people who work in government, in part because innovation isn't prized. In business, failure is often seen as a natural cost of setting ambitious goals, whereas in government, failure is too often seen as . . . well, just failure. Sometimes government can't take risks because people's lives and their well-being are on the line, but there are plenty of times when government operates on pure inertia. When government isn't committed to active innovation, it hampers our ability to create new programs and incentives that will improve Americans' lives.

Still, there are a few inspiring examples of innovative government programs that have promoted entrepreneurial behavior. One is the groundbreaking Bayh-Dole legislation of 1980.

In the late 1970s, the federal government was investing upwards of $75 billion annually in research and development. This investment was hugely successful in that it enabled universities and nonprofit organizations to fund programs, undertake experiments, and develop numerous inventions, formulas, and patents. But out of the many thousands of patents that emerged from all that government funding, less than 5 percent was actually used to produce something commercial. In essence, research institutions were producing amazing innovations that were then stored away in government filing cabinets.

This made no sense at all. Why pour all that money into research if you're not going to use its fruits? That was the question asked by two senators from opposite sides of the aisle, Democrat Birch Bayh of Indiana and Republican Bob Dole of Kansas. Together they sponsored the Patent and Trademark Law Amendments Act of 1980, which allowed institutions to commercialize innovations that came out of government-funded research. Bayh-Dole was a classic example of a successful marriage between the public and private sectors, one that had real-world benefits. As the

Economist magazine later noted, it was "perhaps the most inspired piece of legislation to be enacted in America over the past half-century."

Other great examples of government programs with an entrepreneurial focus are those created to fight rare diseases, such as the Rare Pediatric Disease Priority Review Voucher Program and the Neglected Tropical Disease Priority Review Voucher Program. These programs are organized around a brilliantly devised system that incentivizes drugmakers to invest in treating diseases they would otherwise ignore.

Tropical diseases are a huge problem worldwide, but because they mostly affect poor populations, there's little financial incentive for drug companies to develop cures. These two voucher programs changed all that. The idea behind the programs is simple. If a drug company comes up with a product that treats or cures one of a list of specific tropical diseases, the Food and Drug Administration will allow that company to jump the line for FDA approval on another drug of the company's choice. This is a tremendous incentive, as being the first to market with a new drug typically leads to a huge financial payoff. And the beauty of this setup is that everybody benefits—people, companies, and the government—and without costing taxpayers a dime.

I didn't come to my new career in politics believing that there's one magic solution to the myriad problems faced by a country as large and complex as ours. But I do believe that in the fight to improve people's lives, we must engage every sector of our society. In my travels across the United States, I've found that the strongest communities have something in common: they've created situations where government, the nonprofit community, and the private sector are all working well together. When these three stakeholders work toward a common cause, the outcome is almost always good for everyone.

As a Democrat, I believe that government should play an active role in improving people's lives—but it can't, and shouldn't, do it alone. Right now, government faces three enormous challenges: it lacks the funding needed to drive transformative change, it is not great at innovation, and it is not particularly good at providing the transparency and metrics that give us positive feedback loops.

So how can we in government enlist the other stakeholders, that is, nonprofit organizations and the private sector, to fill in these gaps and help solve real-world problems? One way is through an innovative program called Pay for Success financing, or social impact bonds. Earlier, I briefly described how this approach works in a pre-K program in Utah, but let's take a close look at another area where this kind of financing has made a difference: health care.

ASTHMA IS ONE OF THE BIGGEST HEALTH PROBLEMS AFFECT-ing America today. More than twenty-five million Americans suffer from it, and asthma attacks result in two million emergency room visits a year. Our kids miss fourteen million days of school each year because of this disease; it's the number one reason young students stay home. It also causes American adults to miss ten million days of work, costing our nation $60 billion a year. Unfortunately, these numbers are bound to rise because, according to the Centers for Disease Control and Prevention, the number of sufferers in the United States is continuing to grow.

Asthma also disproportionately afflicts poor people. Many of those who suffer from asthma are covered by Medicaid, the government's health care program for the poor, which takes a big financial hit when someone repeatedly goes to the emergency room for asthma attacks. So asthma is not only a serious health problem but also a fiscal problem for the government.

What makes this even more frustrating is that 40 percent of asthma attacks are triggered by elements in the home, things such as mold, pet hair, insects, and chemicals. Treating these attacks in emergency rooms costs us on average $10,000 per year per kid, but the data suggest that if the government were to invest $2,500 or less to remediate sufferers' homes, we could drastically lower the number of episodes. Paying $2,500 to cut a $10,000-a-year expense in half is obviously an excellent return on investment, but that doesn't mean it's easy to come up with government funding. Medicaid is a federal program, so states don't have the incentive or the flexibility to fund innovative new solutions to a problem like this one. Why? Because the savings from better outcomes would go mostly to the federal government, a disincentive often called the "wrong pockets" problem. Meanwhile, innovation at the federal level faces a different problem: there's little incentive for someone sitting behind a desk in Washington to sign off on a new, untested idea because they're afraid that if it fails, they'll get blamed.

How, then, do we encourage innovative investments in programs that will reduce the number of asthma sufferers? By enlisting nonprofits and philanthropists to work with the government. This idea was pioneered in the United States in Fresno, California, which has one of the highest asthma rates in the country.

First, a nonprofit organization takes over managing the environment in sufferers' homes. They clean the houses, bring in exterminators, fix leaks, treat mold—anything that will mitigate or eliminate the usual triggers of attacks. They also post reminders in the home for residents to use inhalers and take their medicine, and even make calls to ensure that people are doing so. They do all this at absolutely no cost to the government—and this is where Pay for Success comes in.

The nonprofit agrees to do this work without a payment from the government for a set period of time—say, five years. If, at the end of that five-year period, their efforts have resulted in a reduction in hospitalizations and costs associated with asthma episodes, the government then makes a lump-sum "success payment," one that more than covers all the nonprofit's costs but is still calculated to be an overall savings for the government. The net result is a classic win-win-win: the nonprofit gets paid, the government saves money, and, most important by far, the number of asthma attacks declines.

Where does the nonprofit get the money to do all that work for five years? The answer points to another important innovation: the nonprofit issues something called a social impact bond to an "impact investor," a person who wants to invest money in programs that produce a social good. The impact investor—say, the Gates Foundation—buys the bond, providing all the capital needed for the five-year period. If the nonprofit hits its numbers, the government makes the success payment, and the investor gets back the investment plus a return.

Imagine making a donation to a nonprofit, achieving the good outcome your donation was intended for, and then getting your money back. That's what social impact bonds do. If you look at a pie chart that depicts people's spending, philanthropic donations represent only a small sliver. But if you create a category of philanthropy that also acts as an investment, people will be incentivized to donate more, which will in turn make that sliver a whole lot bigger.

I like these Pay for Success contracts for many reasons. One, they get investment capital into a system that needs it. Two, they spur innovation, new ideas, and measurable data. And three, they are fiscally conservative: the government pays only if a contract gets results, which is about the most conservative position you can take.

Pay for Success financing actually represents a perfect fusion of conservative and progressive ideals. If you ask a progressive how to solve the problem of asthma, he will probably say the government needs to step in with more resources. Ask a conservative, and she is likely to resist the idea of a government program, because in her eyes government is wasteful and doesn't get results. But results are the cornerstone of this program, so it appeals to both sides—which makes it a perfect example of the kind of bipartisan efforts we need moving forward. This isn't big government or small government; it's *smart* government.

Asthma is just one of countless social problems we can address through these kinds of programs. Recidivism is another. When people get out of prison, they often have trouble integrating back into society. In many cases, they have no money but can't get jobs because of their criminal records, a dilemma that quickly leads them back into a life of crime. The frequency with which former prisoners relapse into criminal behavior is one of the many reasons we need comprehensive criminal justice reform. In the absence of such reform, though, new social impact programs are helping people manage their post-prison lives, which helps not only the former prisoners but the government and society as a whole.

As with any new program, there are pitfalls. For one thing,

there's the possibility of mismatches in negotiations between the government and savvy investors, because the bigger such programs get, the more likely it is that bad actors will enter the picture in an attempt to rip off the government.

To address this and other problems, I have introduced bipartisan legislation that will make it easier for the federal government to make success payments when savings are accruing to it, rather than to the state or local government—thus solving the "wrong pockets" problem. My legislation also anticipates the negotiating mismatch between government and experienced investors by providing $100 million in grant money for expertise, to make sure these deals are structured in a way that is fair to all parties. If a state administrator goes to a conference, hears about these programs, and then decides he or she wants to start one, we don't want a bunch of shady operators to swoop in and try to get a piece of the action. With this grant money, local governments can afford to hire experts to help them navigate the process. I'm proud to say that this bipartisan legislation, which first passed the House in 2016, finally became law in 2018, and I'm looking forward to seeing how states and local government use this new model to innovate and improve outcomes across the country.

Entrepreneurial ventures can be profitable, and incentive-based solutions can be transformative, but you must always remain flexible and keep an eye out for potential pitfalls. That's a lesson I learned well during the biggest market catastrophe of the century, the financial crisis of 2008.

AFTER CAPITALSOURCE WENT PUBLIC IN 2003, WE CONTINued to grow the company. As an entrepreneur, I always liked focusing on new ideas and growth, but at the same time I took my job as a risk manager for the company very seriously. The way I saw it, we had a lot on the line every time we made a new loan, and I knew that the livelihoods of thousands of employees and clients could be at risk if I made imprudent business decisions. For that reason, we had some of the highest capital levels for any company our size, an extra margin of safety that helped me sleep at night.

A few years after our IPO, I started noticing some strange behavior in the markets. When we had first started selling debt in the capital markets, the process of completing a debt sale (also called a securitization) was arduous. I would spend weeks at a time going on road shows, sitting down with investors all over the world and taking them through intricate details about my company and the assets we were pledging as collateral. The deals we made were meticulously structured and carefully underwritten by the buyers of our debt—mostly pension funds, insurance companies, and banks. Understandably, they wanted to know everything about us.

With each passing year, though, these transactions became easier to arrange, and not because our company was earning a reputation for prudent lending. Little by little, the investors stopped doing their homework, and then a whole new type of investment emerged, CDOs (collateralized debt obligations), which were pools of capital set up with the specific intention of buying debt like ours.

The managers of these CDOs didn't perform anywhere close to the kind of due diligence the buyers of our debt had done in the past. These "hot money" investors were looking only to make a fee by repackaging the debt they'd purchased from us with all kinds of other debt and then selling it to other investors, many of whom were also investing in CDOs. Selling our debt used to take weeks; now we were selling it practically overnight, and the market was starting to feel like a giant Ponzi scheme.

By early 2007, I was getting very nervous about the market's behavior. Plenty of smart people tried to reassure me, saying, "Don't worry—it's easy money." But as I watched this kind of behavior spread throughout our financial system, it looked too much like storm clouds for me not to take cover.

I decided to take action. In order to mitigate our risk in the event of a full-fledged market meltdown, I initiated the process of buying a California-based deposits-only bank called Fremont Capital. If the stock market collapsed, we could use those bank deposits to continue to fund our loans to small businesses.

That seemed like a good start, but I had a feeling it wouldn't be enough. Yet when I called a meeting of CapitalSource's board and told the members that we needed to raise more capital, many of them pushed back hard. The share prices of almost all financial firms had already started to fall, and ours was no exception, having dropped from a high of $27 the previous year to about $17. Under normal circumstances, this would have been a bad time to sell more stock. And as my board reminded me, we already had $3 billion in real capital in the company and higher capital levels than any of our peers. We were prepared for whatever was going to happen, they argued, so we should just sit tight.

One afternoon, I had a difficult phone call with a board member who'd been with us from the beginning. His firm owned several hundred million dollars of our stock, and he was taking heat from others at his company because our share price had fallen. Selling more shares in order to have more cash on hand was the last thing he wanted to see happen; he knew that diluting the stock would send the price down further, and he was arguing vehemently against doing it.

I understood why he and a number of other board members were against my plan, but I remained certain that we had to carry it out. "If things get really bad, we are going to need more capital—and there won't be any capital to raise," I told him. "I'm sorry, but as CEO, I have to do this. I think we're going to need this money." I assured him that I would shoulder the blame if this turned out to be a bad decision, and we ended the phone call.

Over the next couple of weeks, I managed to persuade the board to sign off on my plan, and by the summer of 2007 we completed a convertible debt deal that raised $300 million in additional capital. A little more than a year later, Lehman Brothers declared bankruptcy, which marked the beginning of a devastating market collapse and a global financial panic. The crisis was far worse than I or anyone ever could have imagined, ultimately wiping out trillions of dollars in market value, destroying people's retirement accounts, decimating the housing market, and putting hundreds of companies out of business. As with other financial companies, CapitalSource's stock took a beating, but unlike other nonbank financial companies, we had exceptionally high capital levels and we'd diversified into deposit funding. We were also sitting on billions of dollars in cash. That pile of money is what saved us, and we needed every penny of it.

Our largest independent competitor, CIT Corporation, filed for bankruptcy. And this crash, unlike others, didn't spare the really big financial firms: in fact, of the twenty largest ones in the

United States right before the crisis, nineteen either failed or needed an infusion of government bailout money to survive. What was frustrating about this was that some of the biggest financial institutions in the country took cheap money from the government and then aggressively pulled credit lines from their borrowers (people like us), which was expressly not why the government had given them financing. Some of these big institutions tightened CapitalSource's credit lines, although we were fortunate to have a few large banks, such as JPMorgan, stand by us. But for many of the big financial institutions, it was "heads I win, tails the taxpayer loses." This is a major reason that I've been such a strong supporter of the regulatory framework put in place by the Dodd-Frank Wall Street Reform and Consumer Protection Act, and I will continue to fight for its enforcement and strengthening.

Even when our stock price plummeted, we were determined to recover without government funding, which would have been available to us through the Troubled Asset Relief Program (TARP). We had to just grind it out, loan by loan and deal by deal, as we always had, and pull ourselves back from the abyss. In the end, we were one of the only financial companies of our size that was able to survive the 2008 crash without government assistance. And we didn't just survive: even when things were at their bleakest, we continued to finance our clients, and we emerged from the crisis a stronger company.

SUCCESS IN MANAGING ENTREPRENEURIAL ENTERPRISES comes from being able to pivot, whether that means scaling new heights or avoiding pitfalls. And to my mind, this kind of thinking can lead to great advances and clear benefits at all levels of society.

So how can we encourage a more entrepreneurial America? Here are some steps I believe we should take that would help.

1. **Pursue policies that encourage and enable people to take the risks that accompany entrepreneurship.** Not everyone is as fortunate as I was when I took the leap in 1989. When I left the law firm in DC and bought that first home health care company, April had a good job with benefits and could support our young family. We need to ensure that people don't feel trapped in their jobs. If people's health care and retirement aren't tied to employment, they will feel more secure and more inclined to take the plunge into entrepreneurship. In addition, as part of this new social contract, we need to start providing relief on student debt burdens. Otherwise, more and more young people will feel too encumbered to start new businesses. Why should our government make a profit off student loans—and it's making a huge profit—and why should student loan debt be the only debt not dischargeable in bankruptcy?

2. **Put more money into research and development, particularly if we want to continue to be an entrepreneurial country.** Putting resources into basic research is the single best investment our country makes in terms of economic multipliers, and the private sector's increasing focus on short-term returns means that it's less likely to invest in the type of speculative inquiry that's associated with most basic research. In energy, information technology, life sciences, and other fields, we need a transformative increase in investment in basic research that will spur new business formation

and allow us to best our global competitors over the next several decades.

3. **Institute a higher capital gains tax rate for short-term investing and at the same time provide very low rates for people who hold their investments for ten years or more.** What we need in this country is more investment in start-ups and infrastructure, two asset classes that have long-term time horizons regarding when investors receive a return on their investment. What we don't need is more trading and more leveraged buyouts. Though I have nothing against either of these, we should not be encouraging them by way of the tax code. If, for instance, we made the capital gains rates the same as ordinary income rates for the first five years, and then reduced the rate to 25 percent for years five to ten, and then reduced it to 10 percent thereafter, we would change the orientation of investors toward the behavior we want to encourage: investing in new businesses and new infrastructure projects.

4. **Eliminate duplicate and pointless regulations that serve as major stumbling blocks for businesses.** It's not that we're regulating things we shouldn't be, but we are creating massive amounts of red tape through unnecessary and duplicate regulations, which are hurting small to midsize businesses—something I saw firsthand in my own companies. A big business can handle these regulations by hiring a team that spends all its time dealing with them, but small businesses can't afford to do the same, and, as a result, they find themselves at a competitive disadvantage. As president, I would spearhead a regulatory relief bill to help alleviate this

problem and make agencies more responsive to their customer, the American taxpayer.

I'm convinced that taking these four steps will help Americans, and our government, become far more innovative. I'm also convinced that if we don't learn how to become more innovative, our economic system and our very democracy will soon be at risk.

CHAPTER 7

See Both Sides

Courage is what it takes to stand up and speak.
Courage is also what it takes to sit down and listen.

WINSTON CHURCHILL

ONE MORNING A COUPLE OF YEARS AGO, I WAS SITTING IN A meeting at the Cannon House Office Building with about two dozen of my fellow Democrats. The conference chair had invited all of us to a roundtable discussion on how to structure an upcoming caucus retreat in Philadelphia.

These kinds of retreats, which we have every year, involve going offsite for a few days to discuss strategy and the party's direction. I had some ideas for how we might organize the retreat differently, so when the chair asked for comments, I spoke up. "Here's what I would do," I told the group. "Let's have one whole day where we bring in Republican strategists and policy people. Wouldn't it be interesting to hear how they think about the world and what they're advising Republicans to do?" People looked at me like I was from Mars.

I tried to explain. "Look, these retreats basically turn into a bunch of sessions where we all sit in a room together and listen to people we already agree with," I said. "Why not find out what the other side is thinking?" More blank faces. I obviously wasn't making any headway, so I told them about how we had addressed a problem that cropped up while I was CEO of CapitalSource.

In 2005, about two years after our IPO, short sellers began sniffing around the stock, apparently believing it was overpriced. (For those who don't follow the markets: Most people buy a stock and expect that its price will go up, but a short seller borrows a stock and sells it with the expectation that its price will go *down*. If the stock does indeed go down, the short seller buys it at the lower price, returns the stock to the lender, and pockets the difference.) Short sellers target companies they believe are overvalued, and often they'll put out information, whether grounded in fact or speculation, that they hope will drive down the share price. For obvious reasons, short sellers aren't very popular among people who run companies.

At the time, our stock was doing really well, and Jason and I were feeling good about the direction of our company. So I was surprised to learn that the shorts were targeting us; nothing like that had ever happened in my business career. I called a meeting with our senior management team. There was a lot of muttering and groaning around the table, with people saying the shorts were just trying to damage our business to make money. That could well have been true: short sellers often don't care about a company's fundamentals or long-term prospects, as long as they see a short-term opportunity to make money.

The more I thought about it, though, the less sure I was that in our case the short sellers were merely behaving like predators. "Maybe they see something we're missing," I told the team. There was only one way to find out: by asking them directly. I decided to undertake what I ended up calling my "Running at Criticism" tour.

I made appointments with about six short sellers, then traveled to New York and Boston to spend a couple of days meeting with them. They were pretty surprised; CEOs of targeted companies don't normally drop by for a visit. It wasn't hard to see why: most of the meetings were kind of awkward, because although the shorts were trying to be polite, they weren't shy about telling me everything they didn't like about my business. I understood that it wasn't personal, though, and I encouraged them to tell me straight up what their issues were.

I learned a lot from these conversations. Some of the problems stemmed from the way we had been presenting our business. Also, a few short sellers had reasonable concerns about the condition of the capital markets, which turned out to be early warning signs of the coming financial crisis. Some told me they thought the markets were getting too frothy and that we were growing too fast. I considered these legitimate worries and appreciated hearing them. Short sellers aren't by nature evil people; many of them identify real problems with overvalued companies. In fact, it was short sellers who discovered the massive fraud at Enron back in 2001.

These meetings also gave me the opportunity to correct some misconceptions about our company and help the shorts understand us a little better. I realized that by simply showing my face, I had probably made a difference in how they perceived CapitalSource. Just as it's easier to be casually cruel in anonymous online forums, it's easier to disparage a company or organization when you don't know the people running it.

My Running at Criticism tour turned out to be a success, and that's what I tried to convey to my fellow Democrats when I suggested it would be useful to invite some Republicans to our upcoming retreat. In the end, I couldn't persuade them, but I still believe that listening to both sides is the best course of action.

Understanding different points of view remains an enormous challenge for anyone working in politics today. We also need to recognize that not everyone has extreme views. In the 2017 U.S. Senate race between Doug Jones and Roy Moore, for example, Jones won 76 percent of people who self-identified as moderate, whether they were Democrats, Republicans, or Independents. These are the voters we must capture in order to keep winning elections. So the question for the Democratic Party is: What's the best way to communicate with, and win over, these voters? And my question is: If you're a Democrat, why not make a genuine effort to discover what Republican voters care about? It makes no sense for us to hide in our own bubble and put our fingers in our ears when we can learn something from the other side.

SOME PEOPLE HAVE A GIFT FOR LISTENING AND COMMUNIcating, but many of us respond to certain phrases or ideas with little more than a knee-jerk reaction. This kind of communication isn't very useful, as all it does is close us off from new ways of thinking about the issues.

In late 2017, I met with a group of Democratic Party activists in Mason City, Iowa. One of them told me straight up that "any

Democrat who will not commit to a single-payer health care system is not going to get my support."

"So let's talk about that," I said. "This is going to take a little time, because health care is a conversation that *should* take a little time." I took a few minutes to explain my concerns about a single-payer system—in my view, costs would rise too quickly, and such a system might actually result in patients having worse care than they would have otherwise. I went on to describe my fix for the health care system, which begins with allowing Americans over the age of fifty-five to get Medicare.

"There's no question every single person in America should have health care," I told her. "That should be the uncompromising values statement of the Democratic Party, but we need to have a really thoughtful debate about how we get there." This point had exactly zero impact. For her, single-payer was a litmus test, and she wasn't willing to hear other suggestions for how we might fix our health care problems—no matter how innovative or effective they might have been.

These kinds of litmus tests are a real impediment to progress, and unfortunately they're rampant on both sides of the aisle. On the Republican side, any use of the phrase "raising taxes" is enough to make politicians apoplectic. In fact, over the last three decades, it's been very difficult for Republican candidates to succeed in the primaries unless they sign something called the Taxpayer Protection Pledge, which is a promise never to raise taxes for any reason. Started by a conservative antitax activist named Grover Norquist, the pledge has become a staple of Republican Party politics. By signing this pledge, Republicans are effectively turning over their vote to a special interest.

Here's how ingrained that antitax mantra is. In 2011, during a presidential primary debate, moderator Bret Baier asked the Republican candidates whether they would support a deficit reduction deal that provided ten dollars in budget cuts for every one dollar in tax increase. For Republicans, this would have been a ten-to-one net gain, a no-brainer, but all eight of the candidates onstage said they would refuse to support it, declaring they would accept only those budget cuts that weren't accompanied by tax increases.

From any angle, this makes absolutely no sense: they might as well have said they weren't willing to pay someone one dollar to get ten dollars in return. This kind of knee-jerk response, while apparently pleasing to party ideologues, is incredibly damaging in the real world. I'd go a step further, in fact, and say that flatly refusing even to consider any new taxes is irresponsible.

Take the gas tax as an example. For years, the U.S. government has imposed a small gas tax at the pump. These revenues go into a big pot called the Highway Trust Fund, which then doles out money to states for surface transportation projects. Ninety percent of our country's roads, bridges, and transit projects are funded in this way—and for a long time, the fund was self-sufficient, meaning the gas tax covered the cost of maintaining and improving our transportation infrastructure.

The gas tax isn't indexed to inflation, however, so the value of the revenue it brings in goes down over time. And because we haven't raised the tax since 1993, a quarter century ago, the Highway Trust Fund now runs at a shortfall, which means that every five years, Congress has to scrape together some additional money to subsidize it. That's more than a little counterproductive, because it's very hard to raise the amount actually needed for the fund when you're fighting like crazy just to plug the holes in it.

A big reason we haven't raised the gas tax, of course, is because of the attitudes behind that Grover Norquist antitax pledge. But if you asked the American people whether they'd accept a small increase at the pump to improve the roads, most would say yes, because that's not the kind of tax increase most Americans object to. Unfortunately, there's a lack of honesty over this issue, and it gets spun on a partisan basis. As a result, the country suffers.

Again, I don't want to single out one party: Democrats have a similar knee-jerk response to certain issues. For example, it's just as absurd to suggest that no taxes should ever be cut as it is to say that all taxes should be cut. The right answer is we need to be rigorous and open-minded about how we approach policy. We need to see both sides and look squarely at the facts.

ANOTHER ISSUE THAT SPARKS PREPROGRAMMED RESPONSES by each party is Medicaid. Many Republicans want to cut the program, which I believe is immoral, as Medicaid is the only way most poor Americans can receive health care. In fact, it should be expanded. Some more thoughtful Republicans argue that we should reform the program, and while that, to my mind, is the better solution, many Democrats refuse even to consider the idea.

Medicaid is the largest health care program in the United States, and it's far from perfect. It covers only about 80 percent of health care costs incurred, and because it doesn't pay very well, many doctors refuse to accept it. Not only are there some subpar providers in the system, but the population Medicaid covers is also difficult to serve. For a variety of reasons, including the fact that they often work jobs with irregular hours, poor people generally aren't as diligent as they should be about taking medications; nor are they as able to take the behavioral steps needed to help prevent illness. As a result, costs are high.

As this list of problems makes plain, Medicaid needs reforming. Some of the fixes proposed by Republicans, such as giving the states more flexibility to deal with their own programs, aren't bad, but because these fixes are proposed by Republicans, Democrats don't want to hear about them. Right out of the gate, we run smack into that same knee-jerk reaction: Democrats instinctively reject state control, while Republicans instinctively reject federal control.

The way Medicaid currently works is that the federal government puts up between half and three-quarters of the money, depending on the state, and the states put up the rest. The federal government puts restrictions on how to run the program, and the states actually run it. Under Medicaid expansion, which was a central part of the Affordable Care Act, the federal government increased its funding to 100 percent in the first year, an effort to encourage states to expand the number of people covered. Over the next nine years, the percentage paid by the government gradually drops, though it still remains higher than the federal Medicaid match.

As part of their reform efforts, the Republicans have been attempting to pull back that expansion. They dress it up by saying that they're only trying to give states more control, and although they're right that we should give states more authority to do certain things, that's not a reason to cut back the expansion. Our nation can afford to provide health care for our poor, and we shouldn't be cutting it.

Not surprisingly, we end up with another stalemate, with Democrats opposing reform and Republicans opposing expansion. Yet compromise is within reach. Why not cut a deal that allows states to innovate on ways to save money while still providing the same or better quality of care, and then let the states, rather than the federal government, keep the majority of the savings? This would give both sides something to claim as a win, and ideally it would lead to Medicaid dollars being spent more efficiently, delivering higher-quality health care to poor people.

Effective, tough-minded leadership can help us reach just this sort of compromise. We need to take a hard look at the facts, acknowledge that there are good arguments on each side of the aisle, and try to find the best ideas no matter where they reside. Unfortunately, the bases aren't interested in compromise, and our leaders too often play to their party's base. And that, in a nutshell, is the problem with our government today, and it's why Congress accomplishes so little. We argue and we posture and we point fingers, and the American people pay a huge price for our inability to solve the many problems our nation faces. The parties may win, but the country loses.

IMPROVING PROGRAMS SUCH AS MEDICAID—OR, MORE TO the point, improving people's lives—is the reason I decided to enter politics. I was fortunate enough to have found success doing something I loved, and I took great satisfaction in building my own businesses while helping others grow theirs. In the process,

I made a better living than I could have dreamed of as a young boy scraping paint in Wood-Ridge, New Jersey. There wasn't an obvious reason to walk away from my career; in fact, many of my friends and colleagues were shocked that I was even considering it. But I felt the pull of something larger.

My family is Irish-Catholic, and although I grew up in the Church, I'm not the sort of person who speaks easily of my faith. At Georgetown, a Jesuit school founded on the principles of St. Ignatius of Loyola, one of the mottoes is "People for Others." Both April and I feel that service to others is an important part of our faith, and we try to reflect that in our lives.

The parts of the Catholic Church that speak most powerfully to me are its core mission of taking care of the poor and its strong commitment to social justice. April and I are deeply involved in our parish, the Archdiocese of Washington, and we've had the honor of serving on the boards of some great organizations. We wanted to do more, though, and we knew that if I could win a seat in Congress I would have a chance to help improve people's lives on an even greater scale.

April and I talked a lot about what it would mean for our family if I ran for office. Politics can be a nasty business, and we knew that being in the public eye can have real drawbacks. But what propelled us both was a strong desire to do whatever we could to help bring the country back together. Real reform doesn't happen in a vacuum, and unlike many in Washington, our close friends were almost evenly divided between Republicans and Democrats. So April and I decided to do whatever we could to bring together people from both sides of the aisle in the hope of starting a conversation about how to move our country forward.

One way we do this is through our annual Christmas party,

which started out twenty-seven years ago with a country ham, "company potatoes" (reflecting April's Idaho roots), and a keg of beer. That first year, we invited thirty people, and each year since, we've invited more—friends from Georgetown, from work, from church, from our kids' schools, from our volunteer groups. Our goal is to bring together people from every part of Washington, DC: priests, teachers, carpenters, lawyers, members of Congress, kids, and their parents. By now, more than six hundred people come to our party every year, and when they arrive they check their political affiliation at the door.

One person who always attends is Rep. Steny Hoyer. Steny is a long-serving Democrat in the U.S. House of Representatives; currently the minority whip, he is a talented leader and a good friend. A few years ago, he walked through our front door for the party, and the first person he saw was a prominent Republican senator. Seeing the surprise in his eyes, April put one arm around Steny and the other around the Republican, and she steered them both out to the tent erected in our backyard. "This is our Big Tent party," she told the two men. They laughed and got a drink together.

After I was first elected, April and I decided to invite the entire freshman class of the 113th Congress, plus their spouses, to our house in Maryland so we could all get to know one another. When scheduling issues prevented that from happening, we ended up inviting just the Democratic side. Even so, this was a big undertaking, and the security issues involved were more complicated than we'd realized.

We had wanted to keep the party low-key, but the Capitol Police insisted on escorting everyone on the fourteen-mile drive from Capitol Hill to our home, informing us that they had to provide security because so many members of Congress would be traveling together. We went ahead and invited all the freshmen Democrats anyway, but afterward, April sensibly declared that there had to be a better way. Both of us wanted to continue having this kind of gathering, but it was clearly too much of a production to haul people out to our house. So April suggested we get a place on Capitol Hill, which would make it easier to bring people together.

We bought a town house on East Capitol Street, and one of the first big bipartisan events we held there was a presentation by my longtime friend the great entrepreneur Steve Case, who spoke about immigration reform and innovation. Since then, we've offered our house to members on both sides of the aisle as a place where they can hold dinners, book launches, and other events. This is just one more way that April and I try to encourage more bipartisan conversation and activity among our friends and colleagues.

During my first term in Congress, I had the good fortune of being selected to serve as one of the presidents of our freshman class. I partnered with the Republican copresident Luke Messer of Indiana, and he and I soon became friends. Luke's wife, Jennifer, like April, is a lawyer, and the two of them became active in the Congressional Club, a bipartisan club for spouses. Together, the four of us are committed to making every effort to improve relationships across the aisle. It's an ongoing process, made particularly hard by the atmosphere of hyperpartisanship pervading the capital these days, but we are determined to do what we can.

Every year since 1996, April has written a letter to include with our family Christmas card. She writes about what our four daughters have done over the past year, and she includes updates about the two of us, our work, and our extended family. At the end of 2017, she collected all these letters in a scrapbook, and for the first time we looked back through this vivid history of our lives.

Reading these letters, I was once again struck by how beautifully April expresses her feelings on faith and our obligation to serve others. She's much better at it than I am, so I want to include a short excerpt from one of her letters. April wrote this in 2009, and nearly a decade later it still rings true.

> When I began writing this note, my thoughts drifted to years past and I also pondered the years ahead for our family. It is my hope that when writing this letter 30 years hence—God willing—that we look back on these years with pride, secure in the knowledge that we walked that path we were meant to walk with grace . . .
>
> As we are at war, our economy in turmoil and life spins ever faster, may we slow down and think of touching each other in the ways that we can this holiday and for years to come . . .

For both April and me, the desire to open our hearts to both sides, to really listen to what others have to say, and to pay attention to their needs, is rooted in our deep faith. Given the fractured state of American politics today, and the mistrust on both sides, I believe we need to listen now more than ever.

IN OCTOBER 2017, THE PEW RESEARCH CENTER RELEASED A report showing that the partisan divide between Democrats and Republicans was wider than ever. "The gap between the political values of Democrats and Republicans is now larger than at any point in Pew Research Center surveys dating back to 1994," the nonpartisan American think tank found. Over the course of a little more than two decades, on issues such as race, immigration, national security, and the environment, the average opinion gap had increased from 15 percentage points to 36.

Not only that, but respondents from both parties reported that they rarely associate with friends from the other side. Just 14 percent of Republicans reported having a lot of Democratic friends, and a shockingly low 9 percent of Democrats said the same of Republicans.

As one of the study's authors, Carroll Doherty, put it, "The fact that Republicans and Democrats differ on these fundamental issues is probably not a surprise, but the magnitude of the difference is striking, and particularly how the differences have grown in recent years." In the past, Republicans and Democrats differed on *how* to fix problems, but at least we could usually agree on *what* the most important problems were. Now, because of our yawning partisan divide, we can't even agree on that anymore.

This is, unquestionably, dispiriting news. Our problem is that we talk about the issues in such divisive ways, and we're much more likely to reflexively reject what the other side is saying. There's very little rational discussion around ideas and issues these days, and way too much posturing and shouting.

Even so, I believe that deep down we all care about many of the same things. Here are some of the issues I think voters of all stripes—Democrats, Republicans, and Independents—can agree on, and which could make up the foundation of a transformative bipartisan presidential agenda.

- We should make the country as entrepreneurial and competitive as possible, encouraging more start-ups and reducing regulatory burdens that disproportionately hurt small businesses.

- We must solve our country's skills gap. Six million jobs are unfilled because employers can't find skilled workers, even while millions of Americans are unemployed. This is a problem that will only worsen as technology evolves, and we should waste no time fixing it.

- We must invest more in our infrastructure. Transportation systems are the very lifeblood of our country, and we cannot stand aside while they crumble from neglect.

- We must provide high-quality public education that enables our graduates to find meaningful employment or continue their studies. Too many of our schools are failing their students, particularly in our inner cities and, increasingly, in rural America. This growing national crisis demands that we rethink our basic model of education, which was designed in 1892 to prepare students for an essentially factory-oriented economy. We need to update our model to drive more innovation, focus on individualized learning, and ensure that the basic education experience starts at pre-K and goes through either community college or formal skills training.

- We should launch a national service program to unify the next generation of Americans.

- We must craft policies that encourage more philanthropy, more community service, and more investment in solving challenging issues such as disparities in health and education.

- We should practice fiscal responsibility for the long term, and we shouldn't mortgage our kids' future for our own needs. It's worth noting that even as President Trump was signing the 2017 tax bill, which will dramatically expand the deficit in order to give tax breaks to corporations and the wealthy, a majority of Americans didn't support it.

- We are in the midst of a mental health care crisis in this country, and we must address it head-on. Almost every family in America is in some way touched by it, and to continue to allow the health care system not to treat it on par with physical health is an appalling abdication of our duties as public servants. "The pursuit of happiness" should be available to everyone.

- We must solve our devastating opioid and drug addiction public health crisis.

- We should seek solutions to the dramatic escalation in gun violence to ensure that our children are safe in school.

- We should end gerrymandering so that we can return to truly representative democracy.

- We must find ways to ensure health care for every American while also containing our growing health care costs, as this is the most important variable in our long-term fiscal health.

- We need to protect our citizens from the rapid and unpredictable escalation of prescription drug costs.

- We need to undertake effective criminal justice reform. The United States incarcerates more of its citizens than any other country on earth, a tragic situation that ruins lives, costs billions of dollars, and disproportionally affects African American men and communities of color.

- We must revamp the legislation governing telecommunications and artificial intelligence to protect our national cyber-security infrastructure from attacks, and focus on how media affect children's health and well-being, including cyber-bullying, tech addiction, and privacy issues.

- We must ensure access for all Americans, whether in urban or rural areas, to broadband networks.

- We need to ensure that workplaces are free of sexual harassment and gender-based and race-based discrimination.

- We should be investing more heavily in basic and applied research, to drive cures to vexing diseases such as cancer, Alzheimer's, and autism and to drive innovations in carbon-free energy to help combat climate change.

- We must all agree that in a nation as wealthy as ours, no child should go hungry. The current level of poverty in the United States is a national disgrace.

- We must back up our words with action. A truly grateful nation cannot allow its veterans to go homeless and live without health care.

- We need to create a comprehensive national security and defense strategy that will keep us safe from all those who wish us ill, particularly in the context of emerging technologies around weapons systems; to debate a new Authorization for the Use of Military Force; to support our key allies; and to preserve our leadership role in the world.

- We must continue to lead the effort to eliminate nuclear proliferation, the greatest existential threat to every person on the planet.

Our job as legislators should be to identify the best ideas we can find, whether progressive or conservative, and incorporate them into workable solutions. Particularly now, we need moral leadership to initiate an honest conversation about our country and the world. We need a president who can return dignity, humility, respect, and optimism to the American conversation—a president who will stand up to hate and not seek to divide good-minded people. And the way to do this is by embracing, rather than shunning, the other side.

CHAPTER 8

Get Back to Governing

You campaign in poetry. You govern in prose.

NEW YORK GOVERNOR MARIO CUOMO

AT THE BEGINNING OF MY FIRST TERM IN CONGRESS, I learned a lesson about the reality of governing. Soon after my swearing in, I went to a meeting with my fellow Democratic freshmen, an orientation led by a more senior member of Congress. As we gathered in a room in the DNC headquarters, I expected a discussion about strategy and goals for the coming term. Instead, the member essentially told us that although we might have thought we had come to Capitol Hill to legislate, that wasn't true at all.

We had come to Capitol Hill, he explained, to vote with the Democratic Caucus and continue campaigning for the next election. "Don't come in here thinking you're going to do any big legislation," he warned. "You should be spending thirty to thirty-five hours a week raising money and doing the things you need to do to get reelected."

I couldn't believe what I was hearing. I left that meeting resolved to do the opposite, choosing instead to get right to work on an ambitious infrastructure bill.

This was my introduction to the House of Representatives, a place that sometimes seems to be more about perpetual campaigning than governing. When I joined Congress, I wasn't so naive that I believed members spent all their time proposing and passing bills, but I hadn't expected a straight-up directive *not* to do that. I was surprised and dismayed to see how far away we'd gotten from the business of governing and how much the focus had turned to pure political maneuvering.

Admittedly, I didn't know much about the inner workings of politics when I decided to run for public office. The first time I considered running was in 2006, when Sen. Paul Sarbanes stepped down. The idea of running for his seat intrigued me, and April was all for it, but I ultimately decided it was too early for me to leave CapitalSource. When the financial crisis exploded a couple of years later, a part of me wished I'd gone ahead and run for office, as those were some tough days. But after I saw the company through the worst of the meltdown, I started thinking again about public service. People in the Obama administration talked to me about a possible position, but I was more interested in running for office—this time, for the U.S. House of Representatives.

The seat I had my eye on, in Maryland's Sixth District, had been held for nearly two decades by a Republican named Roscoe Bartlett. Representative Bartlett was a conservative stalwart, a member of the Tea Party Caucus, and one of only two Republican House members from Maryland. The other six were all Democrats.

The Democrats in the statehouse wanted another seat, and after the census in 2010 they saw a chance to help make that happen. The census is taken once every ten years, and after it's released, voting districts are adjusted to ensure that each one has a roughly equal population. Maryland's leadership took the opportunity to redraw the Sixth District in such a way that it would include more Democratic voters. This was pure gerrymandering, and it ensured that whichever Democrat ran against Bartlett would have a chance at winning. The fact that Democrats were gerrymandering at all was unusual; in recent years, across most of the country, the Republicans have been shameless about practicing it. That's how, in the past few election cycles, we've ended up with a Republican majority in the House of Representatives even though Democrats have often won the combined popular vote.

By 2011, there were two serious potential Democratic candidates considering the race: Maryland State Senate Majority Leader Rob Garagiola and former Montgomery County executive Doug Duncan. Rob had started campaigning on a preliminary basis, and it was clear he was the candidate of choice for the Democratic establishment. Doug had also begun taking steps toward running, and so, quietly, had I. Then the next draft of the redrawn Sixth District came out, and to my surprise both Doug's house and mine had been drawn out of it.

Was the race over before I could even begin? My house was now one block outside the district, though if I pulled out of my driveway and took a right, I was immediately back in it. Could I still run? I researched the laws and discovered that I could, and then I hired a polling person to find out if residents would be willing to vote for someone who lived just over the line. Fortunately, we discovered that people didn't care so much whether a candidate's address was actually within the lines, as long as he lived close by.

With that information in hand, I had to make a decision. The filing deadline was January 5, 2012, and over the holiday season, April and I went back and forth, discussing whether this was the right choice for me, for us, for our family. Doug Duncan had ultimately decided not to run, and although he'd endorsed me, it was really Rob Garagiola's race to lose. Would I, a political novice living technically outside the district, without the backing of the state's Democratic Party, really have a chance?

We brought the girls into the discussion, too. At the time, Summer was a freshman at Northwestern, Brooke was a sophomore in high school, Lily was in sixth grade, and Grace was in kindergarten. We spent a couple of evenings sitting around the table and talking about what a political career might mean for all of us. Like April, our daughters told me they would be completely supportive if I chose to run. I still wasn't 100 percent sure, but I kept feeling a pull to public service that was hard to ignore. I wanted to use my experience as a businessman to help create jobs. I wanted to use my understanding of the American dream to help kids from the same kind of working-class families I came from. And I wanted to fight for the rights of women, so that my daughters would grow up in a world where they were truly equal to men, free from discrimination, harassment, and bias.

From the outside, the idea that I would run for Congress must have seemed crazy. I loved my work and was making a great living doing it. I had an amazing wife, four terrific daughters, and a full, busy life. One of the blessings of being an entrepreneur was that I had a lot of control over my own schedule, so for years I made sure to be home for either breakfast or dinner. I often drove the girls to school, and I tried never to miss their sporting events or school performances. Our family also traveled together a fair amount, particularly to April's home state of Idaho, where the girls loved to go skiing, hiking, and camping. For me, there's really no substitute for quality family time, and starting a political career had the potential of interfering with ours.

As I was wrestling with my decision, I had a conversation with my good friend Mark Warner, the senior senator from Virginia. I had known Mark for several years, and we became close when we were both members of the Young Presidents' Organization, a group that connects young CEOs. Like me, he is an entrepreneur, and he left a successful career in the telecom business to enter public service, first as Virginia governor, then as U.S. senator. I admire Mark a great deal, so I sat down with him and laid out why I was thinking of running. Then I listed all the reasons why entering the race was probably a bad idea.

When I was finished, Mark responded with a simple but essential question: "How are you going to feel on your deathbed if you wanted to do this but never did?"

I realized he was right. April and I discussed it, and we agreed that we would both regret it if I didn't at least try. And so, on a chilly morning in January 2012, just a couple of hours before the deadline, we drove to Annapolis and I filed my paperwork to run. The primary was ninety days away, and to say I was an underdog would be putting it mildly.

IN THE BEGINNING, I WAS ALMOST COMPLETELY WRITTEN off by both the media and the political establishment. Local newspapers published stories about how I was some rich business guy coming out of nowhere, with plenty of commentary about my lack of political experience. Everyone knew this was Rob Garagiola's seat; he was well regarded; and Maryland's Democratic Party leaders made no secret of their preference for him. But being such a huge underdog also meant I had nothing to lose. So even though I didn't know what the hell I was doing, I jumped right in, hiring a team of people and starting to make appearances around Maryland.

In truth, I was a pretty terrible candidate at first. I'd go to events and give wonky speeches packed with numbers and facts, because that's what I thought people wanted to hear. In business, you get rewarded for knowing all the details, particularly when you're trying to persuade someone to trust you enough to make an investment in your company. I thought the same would be true in politics—that if I crammed my speeches with details, people would think, "That guy seems to know everything! He's got a plan!" Unfortunately, they just thought I was boring.

The first month was pretty rough, but soon my campaign started to turn around. We had very little time—our first hurdle was the Democratic primary, which would be held in April. Fortunately, I'd hired a talented team, and in the early days, when I was raising very little money, I was able to put my own into the campaign. Summer, Brooke, Lily, and Grace jumped right in, making calls, knocking on doors, and marching in parades. April, of course, was by my side every step of the way—and even my mom, who became known in the campaign as the "secret weapon," drove down from New Jersey to make calls and staff the polling locations. "Vote for my son, he's a good man" was her line. Whatever the outcome of our effort, this was ultimately a family endeavor, and I was grateful for their support and proud of their fearless commitment.

Garagiola tried to score points based on the fact that I was a businessman and a political novice, but his arguments lost punch when I got two stunningly good endorsements in March, one from the *Washington Post* and the other from Bill Clinton. While acknowledging that I had no political experience, the *Post* called me "bright, energetic and admired in the corporate world" and declared that I would be "by far the more independent-minded congressman and probably the more effective one, too."

As it turned out, people were also irritated by the Democrats' brazen gerrymandering on Rob's behalf. It was clear to everyone that the Sixth District had been redrawn specifically to favor him, and voters didn't appreciate that kind of manipulation. The momentum started to swing my way, and as primary day drew near I knew I had a good chance of winning.

On April 3, Maryland's Democratic primary voters gave me a stunning twenty-five-point win over Garagiola and the three other candidates in the race. The win gave our campaign a huge boost, and over the next six months we worked hard, kept building momentum, and never lost our edge. That November, thanks in part to another great endorsement from the *Washington Post*, I beat Republican incumbent Roscoe Bartlett by twenty-one points and won the seat. Looking back, I'm proud to say that we ran a very effective campaign and deserved to win, but of course I was also helped by the fact that the gerrymandering had brought a number of new Democratic voters into the Sixth District, turning it from a heavily Republican district to a competitive one.

Even though gerrymandering helped me win my first race, I strongly oppose it. In fact, I spoke out against it throughout that initial campaign, and I wasn't shy about telling voters that I would work to change it. And I did. During my first term, I proposed a bill aimed at ending the practice altogether. Called the Open Our Democracy Act, the bill proposes three steps to reform our broken electoral system.

First, this legislation would make Election Day a federal holiday, so voters wouldn't have to miss work or find time to vote during a busy workday. Have you ever been to the polls at 6:00 a.m. and taken your place at the back of a seemingly endless line of voters? Sorry, but that's no way to run a democracy.

Second, my bill would create a "top-two" primary system for House and Senate elections, which would solve one of the biggest partisan problems we face. Here's how the system would work. Rather than having primaries segregated by party, all the candidates would appear on a single primary ballot, which would be open to all voters. The top two vote getters, regardless of party, would then run against each other in the general election. This system has already been road-tested, too: Washington State adopted it in 2004 and California adopted it in 2010, which is how Democrats Kamala Harris and Loretta Sanchez ended up facing each other in the 2016 election for a U.S. Senate seat. Put simply, this system gives the strongest two candidates a shot to win, rather than having a strong candidate from the state's most popular party face a weaker, or even nonexistent, candidate from the other party.

Under our current system, many states and districts have strong leanings to either the Democratic or Republican side, which means that in many cases the primaries essentially decide the victor. But far fewer voters turn out for primaries, and in many states, registered Independents aren't allowed to vote in them at all. This means that the small and disproportionately partisan percentage of the population that *does* vote in primaries has an outsize influence on who gets elected. And that, in turn, leads to a more polarized and hyperpartisan Congress.

The third part of the Open Our Democracy Act, and the most important part of the bill, would end gerrymandering by requiring every state to create an independent redistricting commission. It makes no sense to allow the party in power to unilaterally redraw districts, because it will always try to redraw them to its advantage. Creating an independent bipartisan or judicial committee would ensure that redistricting wasn't driven by partisan goals.

Gerrymandering is an unusually divisive topic: for obvious reasons, many politicians love it, but the vast majority of Americans hate it. In my view, it's the clearest example of how representative democracy is failing. Moreover, it's worth pointing out that Democrats are usually on the losing end of gerrymandering. Question: Why do we want to keep playing a game we're bad at? Why shouldn't Democrats take the lead in getting rid of this dishonest system altogether?

The problem is that nobody wants to unilaterally disarm. As long as the federal government fails to pass legislation cleaning up redistricting, in most states the party in power is free to do what it wishes. Gerrymandering corrupts our democracy, but because no party wants to give up power willingly, this cynical practice continues.

A president who takes a strong stand on this issue could make a difference. As president, I would talk frankly with the American people about the damage gerrymandering is doing to our country, which would in turn put pressure on members of Congress to take action. It's time to focus on what's good for the voters rather than on what's good for the politicians.

THE DIRTY LITTLE SECRET OF AMERICAN POLITICS, WHICH I saw up close at that initial orientation meeting, is that our political system isn't actually set up to get things done. It's set up to perpetuate itself.

Once you've been elected to public office, there are two ways to get yourself reelected: by accomplishing things or by being a partisan fighter. At the moment, hyperpartisan gridlock has made it incredibly difficult to get anything done. So instead of focusing on the hard work of legislating, everyone has become a flamethrower. Two years after Barack Obama was first elected president, then Senate minority leader Mitch McConnell was quoted as saying he would attempt to block everything Obama tried to accomplish because "the single most important thing we want to achieve is for President Obama to be a one-term president." It didn't matter whether an initiative might help the American people—McConnell was determined to block it for the sake of his party, even at the expense of his country.

This might be a recipe for political success, but it sure makes for lousy governing. The more laws that are passed with the support of only one party, the more our society will be destabilized. In my view, the best way to govern is to give each side at least a partial victory; that way, people don't feel they're hurting themselves politically when crafting good policy and voting for effective legislation. Take my infrastructure bill. We intentionally wrote it so that each side could claim a win. Republicans could have bragged about how they'd fixed the broken international tax system, while Democrats could have bragged about how they were building infrastructure. But hyperpartisanship blocked the bill's passage, and we all suffer as a result.

We also suffer because members of Congress are essentially campaigning 24/7. The skills and objectives involved in campaigning are very different from those of governing, and the balance has gotten completely out of whack. For one thing, members of Congress now spend far more time at home in their districts and far less time doing the actual work of legislating—a trend that started back in the 1990s, under the influence of then Speaker of the House Newt Gingrich. We have persuaded our constituencies that they should expect us to function almost like mayors, going to one event after another, shaking hands, giving speeches, cutting ribbons. But that ought to be the province of local government officials. Think about it. Would you rather have your U.S. representative spending time shaking hands at the county fair or working in Washington to get grants for community colleges and secure funding for improving highways?

This is not to suggest that we should have minimal contact with our constituents—I don't believe that at all—but our job as members of Congress is to represent our constituents in the federal government, and yet somehow we've created this myth that we should spend every possible moment in our districts, and that every moment we stay in Washington is wasted. Even the congressional schedule has changed—and not for the better.

For decades, members of Congress spent the majority of their time in Washington, doing the jobs they were elected to do, and they traveled home to work in their districts only during the weeks Congress wasn't in session. These days, not only do members travel home most weekends, but Congress has actually *shortened* the congressional workweek to make it easier for them to do so. While most Americans work five or even six days a week, our workweeks in Washington last just three and a half days. In a typical week, we'll come to work on Capitol Hill on Tuesday afternoon and wrap up before noon on Friday. And we're off one week every month, and all of August. How many American workers would keep their jobs if they insisted on a schedule like that?

One of my fellow members of Congress, a fabulous guy named Rick Nolan, was first elected in the 1970s. He took a break from politics after a couple of terms to pursue a successful business career, then came back and was inaugurated again the same year I was, in 2013. I call him Rick Van Winkle because, all those years later, it's as if he woke up in a completely new Congress.

I once asked Rick what his job was like back in the 1970s, and he described an entirely different scenario. Members of Congress went to work at 9:00 a.m. on Monday, worked five days, and finished at 5:00 p.m. on Friday. They often moved their families to Washington because it was assumed that that was where they'd be spending the bulk of their time. And their continual presence in DC meant that they were able to engage fully in the complex issues of legislating, spending lots of time inside and outside the office, often with members of the opposite party, discussing and debating the issues. These days, our time is so limited that all we can do is pop in and out of meetings. We rarely spend more than fifteen minutes in any one meeting, which leaves no time for substantive discussion.

Perhaps it's easy for me to make this argument because my district is just outside Washington, DC, and I'm able to go home and sleep in my own bed every night. But if the American people realized how little of our time we actually spent doing what they elected us to do, I can't imagine they'd be very happy about it. For the country's sake, we have to get back to the serious business of governing.

NOT LONG AGO, I WAS IN AUSTIN, TEXAS, FOR GEORGETOWN University's John Carroll Weekend. At this gathering, which is held in a different city every year, Georgetown alumni spend four days enjoying a range of cultural offerings and sharing stories and ideas. The bonds we forge at these get-togethers are often very powerful. April and I enjoyed these long weekends immensely, especially when I was on Georgetown's board of directors and April was the chair of its Law Center, and the school has remained close to our hearts. Both April and I think the Jesuit motto, which says that we should be "women and men for others," is a good way to live one's life, and the school's current president, Jack DeGioia, has animated that philosophy beautifully with his leadership.

I had a couple of free hours that weekend in Austin, so I decided to stop by the Lyndon Baines Johnson Library and Museum for a visit. Walking through the exhibits, I was immediately struck by two things.

One was that just about every piece of furniture displayed had a built-in telephone. Phones were absolutely everywhere: each desk had at least one phone, and some tables had little drawers that pulled out to reveal more. And as historians have documented, LBJ used the telephone constantly. In fact, the museum also offers more than six hundred hours of the president's recorded phone calls, during which he would charm, cajole, and even threaten lawmakers in his efforts to persuade them to advance his agenda.

This leads to the second thing that struck me: the sheer amount of legislation President Johnson was able to get passed. Among many other bills, he signed the Civil Rights Act of 1964, which outlawed discrimination and guaranteed minority groups equal treatment in our country. He signed the Voting Rights Act of 1965, which prohibited racial discrimination at the polls. He signed the 1964 Economic Opportunity Act, which created the VISTA program and Job Corps. During "slower" weeks, he also established the National Endowment for the Humanities and the National Endowment for the Arts, spearheaded the creation of Head Start and the Food Stamp Program, and signed into law an education bill that vastly increased federal spending on our school systems. These laws changed the very fabric of American society, and they all happened under President Johnson's watch.

It's amazing how much LBJ was able to get done during his five years as president. To be honest, it's also humbling and even a little depressing, because I serve in the same body that helped pass all this momentous legislation, and we, by contrast, get very little done. Johnson worked incredibly hard to build support for his initiatives, and in some cases he did it knowing full well there would be political blowback. It's often said that after signing the Civil Rights Act into law, he remarked, "We have lost the South for a generation." Johnson understood there would be dire political consequences, but he never wavered, because he knew that getting the law passed was the right thing to do.

During my time in Congress, however, I've seen lawmakers do the exact opposite. They would tell me privately that they believed a piece of legislation would improve people's lives, and then, in the next breath, they'd say that for political reasons they couldn't support it. Partisan politics infects nearly everything we do, and an especially good illustration of this point is the Social Security bill I'm cosponsoring with Republican Tom Cole.

Social Security, which became law in 1935 under President Franklin Roosevelt, has been a tremendously successful program. In my view, it is a shining example of a smart, progressive policy that accomplishes an important social justice objective. At the time it was implemented, about half the senior citizens in the United States lived in poverty. Over the next fifty years, it helped cut that number by more than 50 percent.

The way it works is simple: people pay into Social Security throughout their working lives, and after they reach a certain age they begin to receive payments back. For more than eight decades, the program has performed incredibly well, with more money going in than coming out. There's nothing about the accounting that's tricky or complicated. If you look at the system like a ledger, we simply need the income line to be equal to or greater than the expenditures line—not always, but most of the time.

True, some years Social Security spends more money than it takes in. If this happens occasionally, it's not a problem. But if, on a cumulative basis, more money goes out than comes in, the system risks becoming insolvent. If that were to happen, we would have to either cut benefits (a horrible option) or move the obligations of Social Security onto the balance sheet of the federal government, which would balloon our deficits and debt (a bad option). And if Social Security were to remain insolvent over any length of time, it would then correctly be labeled an "entitlement" program, as opposed to what it actually is, a "social insurance" program.

During the late 1970s, Social Security ran into serious trouble, and there were a few years when more money was going out annually than coming in. The situation became so dire that by 1981 it became clear that the federal government would need to intervene in order to save the program. President Reagan and Democratic Speaker of the House Tip O'Neill, therefore, worked together to come up with a solution, establishing the National Commission on Social Security Reform, also known as the Greenspan Commission, after its chair, Alan Greenspan, the future chair of the Federal Reserve. The commission consisted of thirteen appointees, a mix of elected officials, actuaries, Democrats, and Republicans.

Forming a commission is sometimes an excuse for doing nothing, but in this case, the Greenspan Commission was a creative solution, for several reasons. First, Reagan and O'Neill knew that making adjustments to Social Security was such a polarizing subject that neither party would be eager to go out on a limb and make suggestions for how to reform it. Handing that task to an independent, bipartisan commission removed the onus for taking action from both parties. Second, the commission was instructed to come up with a proposal to extend the solvency of Social Security for fifty years, but in a way that wouldn't hurt the program. Finally, the president and the Speaker agreed that if the commission came back with a sensible recommendation for how to do that, they would send it to the House for a vote *without allowing any amendments*. That way, they could make sure no one stuck any other provisions into the bill that would politicize it or screw up its passage.

The Greenspan Commission made its recommendation in January 1983. President Reagan responded with the following statement:

Each of us recognizes that this is a compromise solution. As such, it includes elements which each of us could not support if they were not part of a bipartisan compromise. However, in the interest of solving the social security problem promptly, equitably, and on a bipartisan basis, we have agreed to support and work for this bipartisan solution.

Are you surprised by President Reagan's praise of bipartisanship? If so, then you'll be shocked by the statement he made after the bill passed in March 1983.

I want to take this opportunity to express my admiration—and the gratitude of the American people—for the responsible, bipartisan spirit the House of Representatives has demonstrated in its prompt passage of the bipartisan plan to save the social security system . . .

In the months leading up to this critical vote—and again over the past 24 hours—we've seen men and women of both parties and many shades of opinion set aside their differences and join together for the good of the country . . .

Over long months of study, debate, and deliberation—and in close cooperation with the executive branch—a fair, workable plan to save the system was hammered out by the National Commission on Social Security Reform. All of us had to make some compromises and settle for less than what any one faction might consider ideal. But we did it, and, as Speaker O'Neill promised, the House of Representatives has acted promptly and responsibly to pass the resulting bipartisan plan.

That is an achievement we can all take heart from. And I hope and believe it reflects a bipartisan spirit of putting people before party that will guide us all in meeting other national challenges in the days ahead.

"A bipartisan spirit of putting people before party"—that should be a defining feature of our politics. Instead, it's something we're sorely lacking these days.

In the thirty-five years since President Reagan signed the reform plan for Social Security, the poverty rate of seniors has dropped much lower—from 23 percent to about 10 percent. By any measure, the solution Reagan and O'Neill came up with has been a spectacular success, and the lives of countless Americans have been improved.

Social Security recovered and remained financially healthy for decades, but now we're starting to see the same dynamics we had in the late 1970s. The program is still net positive on a cumulative basis, but on an annual basis we've started to pay out more than we're taking in. This is due to the happy fact that Americans are, on average, living longer than they used to. In 1950, we had sixteen workers paying into the program for every person in retirement. Now, that figure is fewer than three workers per retiree. The program's finances are reasonably good for the near term, but the best estimates show that it will become insolvent by 2034—just sixteen years from now. If we make a few small adjustments soon, we can fix the problem. If we wait, the fixes will be vastly more painful. We would have to either cut people's benefits or formally move all our Social Security obligations onto the balance sheet of the federal government, which would drive our debt-to-GDP ratio much higher than 100 percent. Neither option is even close to acceptable.

Representative Cole and I have taken steps toward devising the obvious solution. We're cosponsoring a bill that would mimic Reagan and O'Neill's approach: it would set up a thirteen-member bipartisan commission and instruct it to produce a plan that would strengthen Social Security and extend its life for another seventy-five years. The commission's plan would require a "supermajority" vote, meaning it wouldn't pass without the support of both parties. Once the plan was made public, we would fully debate it in Congress and then have an up-or-down vote, meaning no one could add any amendments.

Our bill proposes a solution that has already proven success-ful. It's also fact-based and bipartisan. Creating a commission would save politicians from having to go out on a politically dan-gerous limb with their own fixes. Since Representative Cole and I introduced the bill, it has been applauded by editorial boards all over the country, both left- and right-leaning. In private, a number of members of Congress have told me that this legisla-tion makes complete sense. Yet most of them then tell me, "But of course I can't go near it." And as a result, we're risking watch-ing Social Security go right off a cliff.

Where did that "bipartisan spirit of putting people before party" go? And how can we get it back? As public servants, we are duty bound to improve the lives of the American people we represent. We cannot be afraid to risk political backlash in order to do the right thing. We are better than that.

CHAPTER 9

Focus on the Future

One's philosophy is not best expressed in words; it is expressed in the choices one makes.

ELEANOR ROOSEVELT

DURING THE YEAR I STEPPED AWAY FROM BUSINESS TO FOCUS on philanthropy, one of the organizations I became very involved with was our daughters' school St. Patrick's Episcopal Day School. I had just sold HealthCare Financial Partners, and rather than jumping right in to start another company, I wanted to focus on my daughters and on how I might use my skills to do our community some good. So I joined the school's board of trustees, which at the time was chaired by a foundation executive named Katherine Bradley.

St. Patrick's, which offers nursery school through eighth grade, is located in a tree-lined neighborhood in Northwest Washington, DC, just east of where the Potomac River flows down toward

Georgetown and the National Mall. The school is surrounded by some of the most coveted real estate in Washington, so a few years later, when Katherine and I heard that seventeen acres adjacent to the campus had come up for sale, we had the same thought: the school *has* to buy that land. This was an exceedingly rare opportunity—it might be a generation or more before a similar parcel came on the market again. Buying the land would allow the school to expand in the future, so, as fiduciaries, we knew we had to advise it. But the hefty purchase price wasn't for the faint of heart.

At the time, Katherine was ending her tenure as chair of St. Patrick's board, and I was the chair-elect. Together, we urged the other trustees to move quickly. Understandably, many of them pushed back; this would be a larger investment than the school could make, so a number of trustees feared that we might be biting off more than we could chew. Several larger institutions, such as George Washington University, were also considering bidding for the parcel, so we needed to act swiftly and decisively—but the trustees continued to debate the wisdom of the move.

One weekend shortly after the land came on the market, April and I traveled to Wintergreen, Virginia, with Katherine and her husband, David. By now, the four of us not only were deeply involved with the school but had become close friends. Our kids knew one another, too—in fact, the Bradleys' son Carter was on a ski team with our daughter Summer, which is why our families were visiting Wintergreen together. While there, we talked about the opportunity presented by the parcel, and all four of us agreed that we had to find a way for the school to make the purchase.

David and I decided to drive back to Washington a day early so we could come up with a plan. As we wound along Route 29, just east of the Shenandoah Mountains, we talked about how to create a workable deal. We understood why the board was nervous, as taking on a new multimillion-dollar debt was a risky step for the school to take. But looking at it with, as David suggested, a fifty-year horizon, we knew the purchase was unquestionably the right choice. David and I spent three hours in the car—him nursing a Diet Coke, me with my cup of coffee—formulating a creative plan that would eliminate the risk for the school.

First, our two families would put up the money and buy the land through an entity we would form called Friends of St. Patrick's. This approach would not only shield the school from financial risk but also put us in a position to get the property for the minimum offering price. Next, to broaden support for the purchase, we would invite a few other families to contribute to the fund.

Now we got to the creative part. We would partner with a developer who wanted a portion of the land, then work with the DC zoning board to get those seventeen acres rezoned into two parcels—ten acres would be set aside for the school and seven acres would be available to the developer to build single-family homes. The work of getting the rezoning accomplished felt like a throwback to my earlier days with Dominic Tucci and the Wood-Ridge Zoning Board, but this time we would hire professionals. Once the property was successfully rezoned, making it possible for St. Patrick's to build a new athletic field, a high school, and a middle school on its ten-acre parcel, we would give the land to the school.

Making the deal wasn't easy, and it wasn't without risk. But by thinking about the long term and acting creatively, we were able to complete the purchase and get the land rezoned, positioning St. Patrick's for growth that would benefit generations to come.

The lesson here is plain: the way to prepare for an uncertain future is through a combination of foresight, creativity, and common sense, and that applies whether we're talking about a family, a school, a company, or a nation.

THE WORLD IS CONSTANTLY CHANGING, AND THESE DAYS the pace of change is faster than ever. More and more countries are joining the modern economy, expanding their capabilities, and making investments in their futures, and as the world gets more competitive, those who fail to adapt will fall behind.

Take China. Through its One Belt One Road policy, China is investing in infrastructure and economic connections at home and abroad, taking clear and deliberate steps to prepare for the industries of the future, and asserting global leadership on issues such as climate change. The hard truth is that even though the United States has for decades been the most powerful and successful nation on the globe, this is no guarantee of success in the years ahead. We have to keep preparing our nation for the future.

Americans of every sort, young and old, rich and poor, are feeling a growing sense of insecurity. Student debt is crushing a generation. Younger Americans are delaying marriage and thinking twice about having children. People without college degrees are staying put, reluctant to move for employment as they did in years past. The opioid epidemic is laying waste to entire communities. We're falling behind in the never-ending race to build a skilled workforce. We feel more isolated in the world and less sanguine about our future. Sometimes it seems as if huge parts of our nation are frozen in place, stymied by the pace of change.

How can we restore people's faith in where our nation is heading? How can we make them feel more secure, so they engage more successfully in society? This won't be easy, but we can do it by redesigning the basic social contract that makes it possible for our citizens to pursue opportunities and by taking steps now that will ensure prosperity and protection in the decades ahead.

This has consistently been my goal with the numerous plans and bills I've put forward. My Social Security plan would implement small fixes today to ensure that the program endures, averting great pain in the future. My infrastructure bill would have a tremendous positive impact on not only our economy but also our lives. My plans for expanding our basic educational pathway to include pre-K through community college would help close the growing skills gap. And the plans I've offered to address climate change, provide every American with adequate health care, and create incentives for more investments to flow into disadvantaged communities would help restore America's strength. My strategy for our budget would ensure long-term fiscal security, and my approach to national security, trade, and global alliances would build on the progress we've made since World War II, helping to make our nation safe and prosperous. If we're going to invest in our future, we must make hard choices and set clear priorities, and the most straightforward way to reflect those priorities is through our national budget.

So let's talk for a moment about the budget.

Right now, about 70 percent of our budget goes to mandatory spending programs such as Medicare, Medicaid, and Social Security. Targeted tax revenues (payroll tax, FICA tax, etc.) pay for most, but not all, of these programs, with the shortfall automatically covered by the government. The payments issued under these programs don't require congressional approval; they're just baked into the budget year upon year. The remaining 30 percent represents discretionary spending, which is the part of the budget that Congress actually approves. About half of this slice is military spending, and half comprises nonmilitary domestic programs, though it includes items such as Veterans Affairs and Homeland Security.

In order to ensure a healthy budget, we need to better balance our tax and spending priorities. Earlier, I explained that establishing a long-term deficit goal of between 2 and 2.5 percent of our annual GDP would guarantee our fiscal strength. Yet, in 2016, the government took in $3.3 trillion in revenues and spent $3.9 trillion, creating a deficit of $587 billion—3.2 percent of our GDP. Because our economy grew 1.6 percent that year, our cumulative debt as a percentage of GDP increased from 74 percent to 77 percent. These aren't good numbers.

Keeping discretionary spending under control is important, but we must also ensure that the 70 percent of our budget that's dedicated to mandatory spending is also kept at sustainable levels. That's a difficult task, in large part because Americans are, on the whole, living considerably longer. That's good news, but we need to find ways to be sure we don't put the burden of sustaining these important programs squarely on the shoulders of younger generations.

Now let's look at how we're currently addressing—or, more accurately, failing to address—this problem. In late 2017, Republicans passed a tax reform measure that significantly worsens our overall fiscal trajectory. While there were certainly some positive aspects of the law, the legislation was crafted to add $1.5 trillion to our projected deficit over the next decade. As a result, the GOP plan will cause the cumulative debt as a percentage of our total economy to jump from today's 77 percent to almost *100 percent* (or more than $30 trillion) in just ten years. That's a level we haven't seen since World War II, and it's clearly not sustainable.

Why did the Republicans pass such a misguided bill? Because they believe in trickle-down economics and claim that their tax cuts will result in a faster-growing economy, which will in turn lead to more tax revenues. Based on their models, the debt will go no higher than about 90 percent. That's not 100 percent, but it's still not great; worse, their models are completely at odds with those of nearly every mainstream economist who has studied the plan. The Republicans, in other words, are in the thrall of wishful thinking, if not outright fantasy.

Making matters worse, in an effort to avoid another government shutdown, the GOP recently negotiated a two-year bipartisan budget deal that adds $300 billion more in spending. If made permanent, this double whammy of tax cuts and spending increases will ensure trillion-dollar (or more) deficits every year; that's at least twice the level that's sustainable with realistic GDP growth, and it could result in a debt-to-GDP ratio of nearly 110 percent within ten years. This reality led me to do something I almost never do: vote against a bipartisan compromise. Being bipartisan doesn't mean signing up for bad deals, such as misguided plans that will increase our annual deficit to over 5 percent.

The truth is, our deficit and debt problem is a bipartisan one, with both sides contributing to the problem. If we don't correct our financial picture soon, our country will be unable to face the challenges and embrace the opportunities of the future, because we will have dumped an unmanageable debt burden onto the next generation. That is immoral.

Lurking in these two deficit busters is yet another danger: they may cause significant inflation, something many economists fear. If they do, interest rates will almost certainly go up, which would increase the federal government's borrowing costs significantly: for each 1 percent increase in rates, the deficit would grow by over $1 trillion.

We have to put our financial house in order. If we don't, our nation's spending will soon be dedicated to a desperate attempt to keep our heads above water, and we'll have nothing left to invest in our future. It's simple mathematics: we must ensure that there's enough money coming in to pay for the social safety net our citizens deserve and to cover military and other discretionary spending. Otherwise, we will either fail to support our older generations or neglect to develop our younger generations. Neither option is acceptable.

What, then, is the right answer? Unlike most politicians, I am prepared to outline a detailed course of action. Here are the steps I would take to achieve three essential goals: changing our tax policy to generate more revenues, investing our resources differently, and slowing the rate of growth of our mandatory spending programs.

But before I begin, we need to remember where we've come from on this issue. Back in 2010, when President Obama was looking for ways to improve our long-term fiscal condition, he created the National Commission on Fiscal Responsibility and Reform (also known as the Simpson-Bowles Commission) to make budget recommendations to Congress. The recommendations put forth by chairs Alan Simpson and Erskine Bowles, however, failed to garner enough support from other commission members to be considered by Congress.

The following year, the Budget Control Act of 2011 created a Joint Select Committee on Deficit Reduction, known as the Supercommittee. This committee was charged with developing a bipartisan plan to trim the deficit by $1.5 trillion over ten years or face large across-the-board budget cuts known as the "sequester." Unfortunately, the committee failed in its mission. Yet thanks in large part to the sequester, the United States reduced spending by almost $4 trillion before the most recent budget deal passed. At the same time, we raised revenues by only around $800 billion, mostly through the partial repeal of the Bush tax cuts. So even though most people don't acknowledge it, we've actually already cut a fair amount of spending, though we have failed to raise revenues in any meaningful way.

I have already put forth a number of proposals for creative ways to generate substantial new revenues. Some (such as my proposed carbon tax, which would generate $1.6 trillion, and the gas tax adjustment, which would raise another $200 billion) I've already described. Here are a few others.

First is a comprehensive immigration reform plan. Since I've been in Congress, one of the great missed opportunities has been the failure of House Republicans to take up the 2013 Senate immigration reform bill. That bill, which had broad bipartisan support, did three crucial things: it increased border security, created a path to citizenship for the eleven million undocumented people living here (including the Dreamers), and reformed our visa program for both high-skilled and low-skilled workers. It was also the right thing to do morally. In addition, independent analysts have shown that the bill would serve as a major stimulus to the

U.S. economy. Not only do immigrants grow our population, a valuable contribution in its own right, but they also contribute heavily to our economy. The equation is simple: the more immigrants who are documented and pay taxes, the more money comes into our treasury. If the House had passed the immigration reform bill, which President Obama would certainly have signed into law, we would have added a projected $200 billion in revenues to the federal government. And here's another benefit: the more immigrants who come to our shores seeking better opportunity, the more entrepreneurs get unleashed. An immigrant is more than twice as likely to start a business as a person born here, and immigrant-run businesses employ about one in ten American workers.

The Republican tax bill set the corporate tax rate at 21 percent, but I believe it should be 25 percent, which would deliver another $400 billion in revenues to the federal government over the next ten years. There's a myth about the previous U.S. corporate tax rate: even though it was officially 35 percent, higher than that of almost any nation we compete with, the average rate our corporations *actually* paid, because of deductions and loopholes, was closer to 22 percent. The U.S. business community had long advocated cutting the top rate from 35 percent to 25 percent, which would have been smart. But the Republicans recklessly cut it even further, which will add hundreds of billions of dollars to our deficit.

We should adjust allowable deductions in ways that would put another $400 billion in our federal coffers over the next ten years, partly through tweaks to corporate deductions. I've also advocated for the Buffett rule, which would implement a minimum tax rate for high earners and would close certain loopholes such as carried interest, generating another $100 billion. If we impose a small surtax on the top tier of wealthiest Americans (those who earn more than a half million dollars a year), we would raise more than $150 billion, which I would allocate for universal pre-K. Also, we should restore the estate tax to its prior levels, which would generate another $200 billion, and we should adjust the FICA tax.

In all, my proposed budget would add $4–$5 trillion in revenue over the next decade. Simply by making creative decisions, many of which have ancillary benefits, we can make an enormous investment in our nation's future. To be clear, I understand why people and businesses don't want to pay higher taxes, and taxes can indeed hurt economic growth. But we need a clear-eyed, forward-thinking tax policy to pay for the programs that will keep us safe, create a social safety net, and invest in our children and grandchildren. We just have to find the right balance.

Now let's turn to the question of how we can better invest our resources. As discussed earlier, we need to invest in universal pre-kindergarten, so that all American kids can get a jump-start on their education. We should make community college free, a relatively inexpensive move that most states are already beginning to implement, and we should invest more deeply in government research in life sciences and energy. We need to implement a national service program, combined with apprenticeships that will help close the skills gap. Our military and diplomatic budgets, which have been strained by the sequester budget caps, need relief. Also, we should expand the Earned Income Tax Credit, as I've already explained, and put the necessary resources into improving our infrastructure: in the decades to come, this will spell the difference between countries that stay on top in an increasingly competitive global economy and those that fall behind. Over time, all these investments will pay tremendous social and economic dividends.

Finally, how can we keep the costs of our mandatory spending (on programs such as Medicare and Social Security) from ballooning out of control? More important, how can we do so without harming or cutting services to the vulnerable populations that receive them? We can accomplish much of this by focusing on health care savings and implementing efficiency measures such as limiting drug costs, creating more competition among Medicare providers, and offering a public option. By slowing the programs' growth rates and finding savings through greater efficiency, we can save an estimated $1.0–1.5 trillion over the next ten years.

This is the foundational framework for my budget plan, and I will make more details available as we draw closer to 2020. At that time, I will also include specifics about my plan to ensure that every American has access to health care, which the current budget does not include. Unlike the Republicans' tax plan, my budget doesn't rely on rosy projections and it reduces the deficit, even though I truly believe that improvements in skills and competitiveness will likely cause our economy to do better than baseline.

I like to say that two things in life are certain: God and mathematics. And my code is simple: I believe in God and try not to fudge my math.

PLANNING FOR THE FUTURE IS NOT SIMPLY ABOUT BUDGETS and ledgers. It's also about learning to adapt, and thrive, in new scientific and technological landscapes. Never before have humans seen such rapid changes in how we communicate, work, and entertain ourselves. How we respond to these changes will determine how helpful, or potentially damaging, they might be.

When I started my first term in Congress, I was shocked to find there was no caucus set up around the issue of artificial intelligence, or AI. This seemed a serious oversight, as the future of AI is now one of the most important issues facing business, the nonprofit world, and academia. Yet, for whatever reason, the conversation about AI was happening everywhere but in government. Over the last decade, politicians have stood by and watched as technology and communication companies converged in ways that have affected numerous aspects of our lives, outpaced our outdated telecommunication laws, and invaded our privacy. And government has simply not kept up to speed with these changes.

The term *artificial intelligence*, coined in the 1950s, refers to a computer's ability to simulate natural human intelligence. For decades, machines did exactly what humans told them to do, but with the advent of AI, machines have started to figure out for themselves how to function. One early example was Deep Blue, the IBM computer that learned to play chess well enough to defeat one of the world's greatest players, Garry Kasparov, in 1997. Two decades later, drones, self-driving cars, and online assistants such as Siri and Alexa are examples of the kinds of artificial intelligence that are expected to become ubiquitous in American life.

It's no exaggeration to say that AI will change the future of almost everything we do. And because we have so little understanding of the technology within the government sector, I founded the AI Caucus in the House as an educational and convening tool. Since the caucus started, we've had companies such as Google and IBM give us briefings, and we've engaged in roundtable discussions so members can ask questions about where this technology is heading. Out of these efforts, we've created a piece of groundbreaking, and bipartisan, legislation.

The bill, called the Fundamentally Understanding the Usability and Realistic Evolution of Artificial Intelligence Act of 2017 (the FUTURE of AI Act, for short), promotes an environment that enables continued development of AI technology. It establishes a federal advisory committee to examine the vast and varied economic impacts that these technologies will have in American life, and it calls for recommendations within eighteen months on how the government and businesses can work together on the issue. If the act is passed, the committee will include a broad spectrum of members, from civil liberties groups and technology companies to data scientists and labor groups, thus ensuring a wide variety of perspectives.

We need to consider many points of view, because we're hearing a lot of conflicting ideas about how AI will affect our lives. Elon Musk, the brilliant entrepreneur behind forward-thinking companies such as SpaceX and Tesla, has darkly warned that AI technology could lead to a time when machines take over our world. Others suggest that even if that doomsday scenario is overblown, intelligent machines will inevitably replace workers, leading to mass unemployment and economic breakdown. One of the most commonly cited examples is easy to imagine: once self-driving vehicles are widely available, tens of thousands of truck drivers, taxi drivers, and delivery people will be out of work.

While some declare that the sky is falling, others prefer to hide their heads in the sand and pretend that nothing significant is happening. There's no question that many people find the rapid pace of change frightening, particularly older people who are more reluctant to embrace new technology, and it's difficult to talk rationally about the issue when it arouses such strong emotional responses.

When it comes to innovation, however, I am generally an optimist. Over the course of human history, innovation has created more jobs than it has displaced. Yet it's hard for us to see that because, as an era of rapid change gets under way, it's more obvious which jobs we will lose. Yes, many drivers will be put out of work once self-driving vehicles become ubiquitous, but other jobs (in logistics, loading, data) will be created. We just don't see these new opportunities for work because they don't yet exist.

In 2017, during a Facebook Live chat set up by the AI Caucus, I talked with Johns Hopkins University computer science professor Dr. Suchi Saria and Google X founder Dr. Sebastian Thrun about this issue. Dr. Thrun was particularly bullish about the idea that AI will create a lot of jobs. His theory is that, as AI technology helps society to enhance productivity and create wealth, we can then redirect it into creating new positions. Why, for example, should classrooms have ratios of twenty-five kids to one teacher? With enhanced productivity driven by new technologies, we can cut that number to ten students per teacher, or even five. Similarly, why should people have to wait in doctors' offices, when new technologies can streamline the medical process so they can get immediate care?

AI does, admittedly, have potential drawbacks. One fear is that when smartphones can use facial recognition to identify our reactions to images, the intelligent computers that power them will be able to create messages aimed at manipulating our emotions or even controlling our minds. Imagine a world in which a remote computer digs up an old video of a deceased parent, then replicates that person's voice with messages designed to influence buying habits or, worse, votes. This is a plausible, and deeply unsettling, scenario.

AI will significantly reshape our economy in the same way the steam engine, the transistor, the personal computer, and the Internet all once did. It will change the future of work and many other aspects of society. These changes are inevitable, so it's imperative that we get our government involved now, to ensure these advances serve Americans rather than harm them.

ENVISIONING THE FUTURE OF AI IS JUST ONE EXAMPLE OF how we must devise a broader strategy for moving our country forward, through 2020 and beyond. We have to recognize the trends of the future and learn to influence them to our benefit. In the end, we cannot stop change from happening; we can only position ourselves to gain as much as possible from it.

One of the most important things we must do is prepare our citizens for the future of work. Technological innovation will improve productivity and help our businesses compete, but it will also have an impact on jobs; according to a recent McKinsey & Company study, in approximately 60 percent of existing occupations, about a third of work-related activities can already be automated based on currently available technologies. And that percentage is destined to grow, because the rate of technological innovation, particularly in automation and machine learning, is accelerating.

New technologies will completely replace some jobs and significantly change many others, and people will have to learn new skills in order to work side by side with machines. While we can't precisely predict how this mix of disruptive and creative forces will affect specific jobs or industries, we can, and must, take affirmative steps to prepare Americans for this future of work. As president, I would focus on several areas to transition our workforce most successfully, including:

- **Providing better skills training.** Georgetown University's Center on Education and the Workforce estimates that between now and 2024, the United States will have openings for sixteen million middle-skills jobs, defined as those requiring some post–high school training but not a four-year degree. Meeting this need will require supporting and maintaining our world-class university system. But we must also put into place new ideas such as national service, free community college or certificate-based skills programs, innovative pay-for-success career and technical training programs for economically challenged communities, and ongoing workforce training.

- **Redefining benefits.** The jobs of the future will be more flexible and more fluid. People will change jobs more frequently, require regular breaks for training, and need to be connected more broadly to work opportunities (Google is currently innovating in this area with Google for Jobs). In addition, more workers will be employed as independent contractors rather than full-time employees. These changes mean we must think differently about the basic benefits packages people need. As I've described earlier in this book, health care and retirement should be decoupled from employment, and every worker should have access to paid family leave.

- **Supporting creativity.** While science, technology, engineering, and math (STEM) skills will be crucial to many jobs of the future, technology will help liberate workers from the more mundane aspects of work, freeing people to be more creative. In addition, enhanced productivity should allow people to have more free time, creating a greater demand for entertainment. Moving forward, we must ensure that basic education in our country allocates time to the arts and other creative endeavors.

- **Encouraging people to work longer.** Thanks to advances in medicine and improved living conditions, Americans are living longer. As people age, their need for health care increases, creating a greater demand for nurses and health care aides, which means we need more programs oriented toward training these workers. In addition, available data suggest that when people work longer, they not only live healthier lives, but also require less support from safety net programs. For these reasons, we must support innovative programs to encourage or incentivize workers to stay in the workforce longer.

- **Supporting wages.** In the future, we're likely to see substantial growth in the types of jobs that don't earn high compensation. The changing nature of work will also keep wages low as the workforce experiences significant disruption. We need to expand the Earned Income Tax Credit, and we must also support higher minimum wages and wage support programs to help ensure a smooth workforce transition.

- **Exploring the marketization of uncompensated work.**
  People often worry that in the future new technologies will
  replace all jobs. While this fear is understandable, history
  shows us that innovation tends to create more jobs than it
  displaces. However, if in fact this time turns out to be different, we should focus on how to use the productivity created
  by that new technological world to compensate people for
  jobs that add value to society, but for which there's no economic model for compensation. Meaning, we would need to
  create innovative benefit and compensation schemes for
  people working as caregivers, mentors, tutors, child care
  workers, and the like.

Globalization offers a vivid illustration of this point. In the
2016 election, globalization was consistently painted as the villain in our economic drama. Candidates such as Bernie Sanders
and Donald Trump vilified international trade agreements, arguing that our decision to become part of the global economy has
harmed American workers. Their solution: retreat from the world
stage. But how can it possibly be wise to decide not to be part of
the global economy? Should we really isolate ourselves, cut off
trade deals, and raise tariffs? This makes no sense, for two reasons.

First, those who argue against trade deals are arguing against
the future. They're fighting to bring back an era in which the
United States didn't trade much with other countries—such as
the post–World War II period, when the United States faced no
serious global competition because so many other nations were
rebuilding. But that world is gone and it's not coming back. It is
simply not realistic to suggest we should wall ourselves off economically from the rest of the globe.

Second, this backward-looking view completely misses the point that globalization has, in fact, been a tremendously positive force worldwide. In 1960, 65 percent of the world lived in extreme poverty, and trade represented 24 percent of the global GDP. Now these numbers are dramatically different: just 10 percent of the world lives in extreme poverty, defined as earning $1.25 a day or less, and trade represents 60 percent of global GDP. This historic turnaround has lifted literally billions of people out of the ravages of poverty, a trend that progressives should applaud. Further, as a result of globalization, the United States has benefited from lower prices for millions of products, a more stable world through the creation of a global middle class, and faster sharing of information and innovation.

Although these impressive numbers show that globalization has been a positive force overall, it's true that many American communities and workers have suffered. Jobs have migrated overseas, workers have been forced to take pay cuts and deunionize based on threats to outsource their jobs, and foreign competitors have undercut U.S. companies, which has resulted in plant closings and business failures. In addition, globalization combined with technological innovation has caused much higher income inequality, as investors and executives have benefited from labor arbitrage and greater efficiencies at the expense of American workers.

The pain of globalization did not have to be this widespread. Tragically, our country failed to take the steps needed to protect workers and communities—steps such as rebuilding our infrastructure to allow distressed communities to compete, providing incentives for private capital and government contracts to flow into communities, and ensuring that people had the skills they needed to succeed in this new technological environment. We should have seen the wave coming. We should have prepared for it, but we didn't.

The real villain, in short, is not the decision to engage with the world economically. The real villain is partisan politics. Our divided political class has prevented us from helping the parts of the country that we knew (or should have known) would be negatively affected by globalization. And as I wrote earlier, the cost of doing nothing is not nothing: huge parts of our country have paid a very high price for government inaction.

Like artificial intelligence, global economic interconnection is the future. Rather than sit back and wring our hands about whether we want to fully engage with the global economy, we must embrace globalization and plan how to use it for our own good. This is one reason I've been a big supporter of the Trans-Pacific Partnership (TPP). I was one of just twenty-eight Democrats in the House who stood with President Obama in his push to get TPP passed. I was one of the deal's early supporters, working closely with the president's talented chief economic adviser, Jeff Zients, to get the TPP approved in Congress. As it happens, Jeff and I are longtime friends, which made the two of us good partners during the debate about TPP in Congress.

TPP was not just the right answer economically; it also would have enhanced our national security. Here's why.

Opening up the Asian market to American exporters is ultimately good for jobs in the United States. How? If the TPP had passed, we would have been the leader of a twelve-nation trade bloc comprising 40 percent of the economy of Asia. TPP would have allowed us to bring down tariffs and trade barriers. It would have made it possible for the United States to export more products, particularly agricultural products, into many of these markets, which in turn would have encouraged more direct foreign investment in the United States. If my large-scale infrastructure plan had been incorporated into TPP, as I argued it should be, that would have been another major benefit. All of this would have enabled us to prepare for a globalized world while also investing here at home.

Of course, any decision to enter into a trade agreement has positives and negatives. It's never a one-way street; you have to give something to get something. At its most basic level, every trade agreement is about tariffs—that is, taxes on the goods coming into a country. If two countries both have tariffs, there's no incentive to trade with each other, but in a trade deal, both sides lower their tariffs to make the flow of goods easier. That's good for the sellers but bad for the companies who had no competition before the imports arrived. At the same time, a trade agreement creates opportunities for people to set up businesses in other places, lowering their costs.

But trade deals alone don't cause pressures in the manufacturing sector. Once globalization occurred, our manufacturing base eroded as countries with lower costs started to compete with us. And since the United States generally has open markets, these trends would have occurred with or without trade agreements. In fact, we have no trade agreements in place with many of the countries that are our largest trading partners.

A carefully negotiated and fully enforced trade agreement can help level the playing field for American companies by opening up markets for our goods and services on equal terms. A good trade deal can also help establish the rules of the road for building a global middle class, protecting workers in other countries, and encouraging environmental standards. And such deals are even more successful when paired with domestic investment programs.

One of the many reasons I supported the TPP was that it's responsive to these issues. But the biggest reason was that we simply can't ignore what is happening in the rest of the world. I believe we must ensure that we are a player on the global economic stage, which is why I also believe that all foreign policy meetings should always involve not only traditional diplomacy but also economic relations.

Diplomacy, alliances, and economic engagement are the tools for putting us in a position to influence global affairs for the better. We want this sort of influence so that we can promote democratic ideals and greater equality, of course, but also because more stability means less global conflict, less damage to the environment, and greater security. Besides, the better the world's citizens are faring, when global poverty is diminishing and the middle class is growing, the more opportunities the United States will have economically. We have a huge interest, therefore, in making sure the world continues to develop in an organized, pro-growth way and that capitalism, trade, and global interconnections continue to prosper.

That doesn't mean, however, that we should embrace trade agreements unreservedly. To be fair, President Trump is right that we haven't always negotiated or enforced these deals as well as we should have. Yes, we should take a hard look at each of our trade agreements, but it would be wrong to abandon them altogether. The right answer is to make sure global interconnectedness works for us.

This brings us to the question of security. As important as the

TPP's economic implications are, the national security implications are just as important. In the seven decades following World War II, the United States has held the enviable position of global superpower. We have been the indispensable nation, the leader that convenes important international conversations and helps maintain global stability. But it will be difficult, if not impossible, for us to hold on to this position if we don't have the necessary economic levers at hand. So while I fully support fielding the most powerful military in the world to ensure our national security, that alone will not get us the results we need.

Take the example of North Korea. Some observers say we should force China to put more pressure on the leadership in Pyongyang. This is a plausible step, as North Korea depends upon trade with China for its very existence. But what levers can we use to persuade China to take a tougher line with North Korea? If we sanction Chinese companies or the country directly but don't have a competitive footing in the markets most important to the Chinese (meaning the rest of Asia), we risk significant retaliatory reaction.

If the United States develops a stronger economic footprint in the Asia Pacific region, we will be in a better position to put pressure on China. But by tearing up the Trans-Pacific Partnership agreement—which Trump did on his very first day in office—we are passing up an enormous opportunity and handing the booming economies of Asia to China on a silver platter.

THE ELECTION OF 2016 UPENDED THE ESTABLISHED POLITICAL order and called into question many long-standing U.S. policies. People began questioning our decision to engage in free trade around the world and our efforts to build and maintain alliances. President Trump's declarations that our alliances were costing us too much money; that we have somehow not benefited from the most successful alliance in the history of the world, NATO; and that nations such as Japan and South Korea should get nuclear weapons were direct repudiations of the way we have long conducted our foreign policy.

I want to be very clear about this: I support the post–World War II model of U.S. foreign policy, which is to engage diplomatically and economically around the world, to create and defend alliances (such as those with our NATO allies, South Korea, Israel, Japan, key Arab allies, and Australia), and to provide a blanket of protection that lessens the need for other nations to build large militaries. We have adhered to this model for seventy years, and while during that time we have made some mistakes, our disastrous war in Iraq being a prime example, overall this strategy has made us safer and more prosperous, and it has produced myriad benefits, not only for us but for the world as a whole. We have an indispensable role in ensuring that it will be maintained and protected from those who wish to see it weakened.

As the world becomes increasingly interdependent economically and ever more connected thanks to modern technology, it makes no sense for us to become isolationist in our thinking. In fact, these trends make it even more important for the United States to take a leadership role. We can't solve every problem in the world, but I believe we should be leading the conversation on how to do so.

Our first option should always be to engage, discuss, and work together with other nations. Yet when our role as a convener and leader doesn't accomplish the mission and the interests of the

United States are threatened, we must be prepared to use military force. How to determine when to deploy our troops is, of course, the big question. People have widely varying ideas about what constitutes an "attack" on our national interest—which is why sound leadership truly matters. We must be able to assess each situation in a clear-eyed way and accurately determine whether military action will make a difference.

This is clearly what President Obama was trying to do when he chose not to respond with military force after Syrian president Bashar al-Assad crossed the red line by using chemical weapons against his own citizens. It is unquestionably in our interest to make every reasonable effort to prevent other countries from using chemical weapons, and President Obama understood this. But when he analyzed the situation militarily, I believe he decided that we could do little or nothing about Assad's monstrous behavior.

I didn't fully agree with that decision. In my view, it was important to show the world that we have no tolerance for the use of chemical weapons. Even if we had responded in a way that didn't put a stop to the atrocities, we should have delivered a strong statement that immoral actions have real consequences. We must be unafraid to act when it's appropriate to do so, though our president must also always be cognizant of the great cost—to our men and women in the armed forces, their families and communities, and our nation as a whole—of engaging militarily. This is the gravest responsibility a president has as commander in chief.

I was recently on a panel with Gen. Stanley McChrystal, the former commander of the Joint Special Operations Command and one of the key architects of our military strategy in Afghanistan. The moderator asked me whether I would be excited or scared by the prospect of sending forces into battle. My answer: neither.

My view is that the decision to send our men and women into battle must be undertaken only with a full awareness of the heavy burden that such a commitment creates. American soldiers and their families have made untold sacrifices while serving our country. No president should ever use military force until he or she has visited Arlington National Cemetery and stood before the graves of the patriots who fought for the ideals of our nation. No president should use military force unless he or she is willing to look a mother or father, a husband or wife, or a child who has lost a parent, directly in the eye and say, "We had no choice but to put your loved one in harm's way."

Our military is the most powerful in the world, and the American soldier is the finest ever trained. But over the past several decades, we have too often let down the men and women in our military. We sent them to fight in Iraq in a war that never should have been ours. Because of Congress's failure to craft a bipartisan long-term budget agreement, we have strained their readiness and capabilities. As one example, the United States has only recently, with the launch of the Department of Defense's Third Offset Strategy, begun the important work of investing in the next generation of technologically sophisticated weapons systems, including those that employ artificial intelligence and robotics. For too long, we have asked, "How much should we spend on our military?" That is the wrong question. The right one is, "What exactly are we asking our military to do?" And once we answer that question honestly, it is our duty to step up and give the military the funding to do it.

Another way we've let down our military is by refusing to properly confront global terrorism. Since the attacks of September 11, 2001, we have relied upon an Authorization for Use of Military Force (AUMF) for certain military engagements. This authorization allows the president to unilaterally deploy "all necessary and appropriate force" against any entity deemed involved in or connected to terrorist acts against the United States. Signed by President George W. Bush just one week after the 9/11 attacks, AUMF was an emergency response to an extraordinary situation. In the seventeen years that have passed since then, we have failed to update it, thereby depriving the American people and our troops of the chance to have an open, honest debate on the scope of our mission to defeat terrorism. That failure is unacceptable.

One last word about our fighting forces. The men and women who serve willingly often risk making the ultimate sacrifice for our safety and freedom. For this reason, we have a sacred duty to honor them, and that includes doing whatever it takes to help them successfully transition back into civilian life. Veterans' issues has been one of my top priorities in Congress, and I have worked on bipartisan legislation to give our veterans access to better health care and to protect them from predatory lending practices. Our military men and women take superb care of our security. We unequivocally owe them the same.

SIXTY YEARS AGO, ON FEBRUARY 18, 1958, SENATOR JOHN F. Kennedy gave a speech at Loyola College's annual alumni banquet in Baltimore, Maryland. Just four months earlier, the Soviet Union had shocked the world by launching *Sputnik 1*, the first satellite successfully sent into orbit, and the U.S. scientific establishment was still reeling from the blow of having fallen behind the Soviets. Nothing less than the future of space exploration and, potentially, the balance of world power were at stake, and Kennedy knew it.

It's unsettling to read his remarks now, six decades later, because however much we might like to believe otherwise, they still ring true. In place of the word *Soviets*, we could insert other nationalities, such as the Chinese.

We have taken pride in our American inventive genius. But too often we have applied it to gadgets and luxuries, while the Soviets intensified their basic research . . .

We have been complacent about our own supposed monopoly of know-how. We have been mistaken about their supposed ignorance. And we have completely failed to understand the crucial importance of intellectual achievements in the race for security and survival.

Kennedy went on to propose the best possible solution to the problem of how to reestablish American dominance.

I do know that the struggle in which we are now engaged will be won or lost in the classrooms of America. The development and maintenance of a modern defensive force is directly related to the scientific talent available. We already know of our lag in satellites, in missiles, in jet engines and rocket fuels, in detection systems and other scientific essentials. Less well known is the fact that an estimated 9% of our tactical bombers have been kept out of service for lack of sufficient technical personnel. Others have simply not been produced . . .

It should be clear, in short, that victory—in the words of Sir David Eccles, President of the British Board of Trade—

"will go to the people with the best system of education—both in the sciences and the humanities."

The structure of American education must be painstakingly rebuilt from the bottom up—with more and better schools, more and better teachers from the primary grades on. The Federal government must be willing to put into the construction of new public schools each year for the next several years at least as much as the cost of one aircraft carrier.

Sound familiar? Then, as now, the United States was suffering from a major skills gap, and it was causing us to fall behind our global competitors. As Kennedy knew, we had to plan for the future or risk falling behind.

Our lag in educational achievements is also costly in the competition for international prestige and goodwill . . .

While we in the United States are unable to produce enough engineers and scientists to meet our own needs, Soviet technicians are pouring into the Middle East, Africa, Asia and even Latin America . . .

America, as Edward Teller has so solemnly pointed out, has already lost the cold war of science. If we begin now, we may regain our position in the 1980s or even the 1970s. But the 1960s are already lost.

Once he won the White House and was inaugurated, President Kennedy wasted no time in exhorting the American people to step up to the challenge. In 1961, he asked Congress for $7–$9 billion in new funding for our space program, with the goal of "landing a man on the moon and returning him safely to the earth." What followed was a decade of dramatic intellectual competition between the United States and the Soviet Union, with the Americans ultimately winning the Space Race when we became the first nation to put a man on the moon.

Yet now, half a century later, we're losing ground in much the same way we were when President Kennedy issued his challenge. Our goal should be to envision the future, recognize the trends that will make the world a different place in 2030, 2040, and 2050, and start taking the steps that will help us thrive decades from now. We must look at where the world is going, not just where it is today. If we do this with an open mind, it will become apparent what policies we need to pursue in order to maintain our preeminent position in the world.

All my policies flow from this way of thinking about the future. And all have one element in common: they are designed not to stop global trends but to bend those trends to help more Americans. This is why bipartisanship is so crucial as we confront the challenges that await us, and why it's so important that we resist the temptation to focus on conflict and instead focus on the ideas and principles we share. As I wrote earlier, we are too busy looking for arguments when we should be looking for solutions.

Americans have no shortage of creative ideas for how to solve our problems. In fact, because of the enormous intellectual capacity of think tanks, foundations, and the international organizations developed in response to the federal government's paralysis, we have never generated better ideas on how our nation can thrive in the years ahead. So why aren't we acting on them? Because our society has become hyperpartisan and inward-looking. When faced with perceived threats to their core beliefs, Congress and our political parties don't want to make compromises—even though the American people have clearly shown that they prefer compromise and bipartisan solutions to all the bickering.

In this, too, John F. Kennedy was ahead of his time. In the final paragraph of his speech at Loyola, he uttered these inspiring words:

> Let us not despair but act. Let us not seek the Republican answer or the Democratic answer but the right answer. Let us not seek to fix the blame for the past—let us accept our own responsibility for the future.

If we can rise to this critical moment in our history and heed President Kennedy's words from long ago, we can create a better future. *This* is the right answer.

The Right Answer

FROM AGE SEVEN TO THIRTEEN, OUR OLDEST DAUGHTER, Summer, was a ski racer. For April and me, this meant lots of early morning wake-ups for practices in Wintergreen, Virginia, and race weekends at other ski mountains up and down the mid-Atlantic. Our race-weekend routine was always the same. On Friday evening, I would drive Summer to the mountain, usually pulling into a motel around midnight. She'd fall asleep in the car, so I'd carry her in, put her to bed, and lay out her gear in advance of a 6:00 a.m. wake-up. Bright and early the next morning, we'd head to the mountain, where Summer would warm up with the team while groups of parents tended the slopes, set up the slalom gates, and prepared the start and finish areas.

When Summer was eight, she raced in the season-ending

championship races at Bryce Mountain, Virginia. Competing in the giant slalom, she was skiing well that weekend, and after the first run she was in second place. She was one of the last racers scheduled to take the second run, and by the time she took off down the slope it was clear she just needed a solid run to take the silver medal.

I was one of the parents stationed along the course as a "gate watcher," monitoring the slalom gates to note when racers missed them. My gate was the last one on the course, and it had a tricky setup; many of the young skiers were missing it, which meant instant disqualification—the dreaded "DQ." Summer came down with a strong run, but, like many of the other skiers, she missed my gate.

After all the racers had finished, I skied to the bottom of the slope to turn in my card. Meanwhile, the timekeepers had posted raw times and unofficial standings, and, according to their list, Summer was still in second place, which would give her a silver medal—a really big deal for her. Summer was practically bouncing out of her skis, a big smile lighting up her face, as I approached. "Daddy, I got second!" she exclaimed.

"Summer," I said, "I think you missed a gate."

"No, I didn't," she said, her smile instantly disappearing.

"Yup, I think you did."

"*No*, I didn't," she insisted. She genuinely didn't think she'd missed any gates.

Gently but firmly, I said, "Yes, honey, you did. It was my gate, and I marked you as a 'DQ' on the card I just turned into the judges." She burst into tears and skied off.

On the long drive home that afternoon, Summer and I talked about how important it is to tell the truth, even when it hurts. I knew she was hurting from losing the silver medal, and I admitted that it was painful for me, too, to have been the one who had to disqualify her. It would have been tempting not to tell her that it was my gate she missed. But, I explained, I told her because it was the truth.

Summer gave me permission to tell this story—one of the few about my kids that I would feel comfortable including in a book. I wanted to tell it not just for the story itself, but because it's about my most important job: being a dad.

LIKE ALL PARENTS, APRIL AND I HAVE TRIED TO RAISE OUR daughters to be good, though it's admittedly hard work and we don't always get it right. I once heard about a survey that asked older parents of adult children whether they had aimed to raise their kids to be "good," "happy," or "successful" (defined in terms not of income, but of being engaged in meaningful and/or enjoyable work). The parents could choose only one. The survey then asked how their kids had turned out. The results showed that children who were raised to be "happy" were rarely deemed, in the eyes of their parents, to have turned out both "good" and "successful." The kids who were raised to be "successful" were rarely both "good" and "happy." But the kids who were raised to be "good" were, more often than not, also both "happy" and "successful."

That said, raising your kids to be good can be a lot harder than raising them to be happy or successful. April and I are immensely proud of our remarkable daughters, now aged twenty-five, twenty-one, seventeen, and ten, and we hope we have served them well as parents. Our daughters have been supportive of our decision to enter politics, which hasn't necessarily been easy for them—particularly for our younger girls, Lily and Grace, who have been at home during our political years. They've seen the campaign ads on television, bought by super PACs, making negative attacks on their dad. Politics is a full-contact sport, but when you have a strong family, as I do, you can fight through it. It helps to know that the people who love you have your back.

April and I have always felt that our most important goal in life was to be good parents, and we've tried to make our daughters the "center of the center" of our life. It's our job to protect them, care for them, be good role models for them, and prepare them for meaningful and independent lives as adults. Parenting is the work we enjoy and value the most. But while the work brings joy, it does take time, which is hard for many people to carve out in a world that grows more difficult to navigate each year. For many parents today, economic hardship, the friction of day-to-day life, and the intrusion of social media into private family space have made effective parenting a tough hill to climb.

April and I have been blessed to be able to spend time with our kids, and we aim to be truly present when we're with them. To go to their games, meets, matches, and performances. To help them with homework (which includes doing crash courses online when they have a question about chemistry!). To have at least breakfast or dinner together each day as a family. To talk about what's going on in their lives and tell them about ours. To have our weekends wonderfully consumed by whatever activities they have going on.

As a good friend of mine likes to say, "You can't fake showing up"—and that certainly applies to parents. I can't remember any problems that might have arisen from missing business dinners or political events, but I can vividly remember the joy of picking up Summer from her chorus practices and sneaking in a slice of pizza from her favorite pizzeria on the way home. Or the fun of embarrassing Brooke by singing in the car with her friends on the way home from soccer practice. Or the delight of messing up the kitchen with Lily as we cooked up something great together. Or the happiness of making it home in time to tuck Grace into bed while making up fanciful stories about her favorite stuffed animals. I'll remember these special moments with my kids until my last breath.

People have lots of theories about being a dad, but the only one I have is my simple rule of being there for them. Because, in truth, there is no complicated formula to good parenting; it just requires time and a set of values to guide you. As parents, we learn from our kids. They teach us that it's still okay to have fun, try new things, dream, and be silly. They remind us that we don't know everything; in fact, we adults often don't know very much at all about how life is unfolding for teenagers. And they remind us that the world is much bigger than we are. Being a good parent, in short, means learning not to be selfish.

I have been blessed with the privilege of trying to live a meaningful life in public service—of being able to fight for the moms, the dads, and the kids for whom life is hard. I know what they need and what they want, because I've been through it too as a four-time parent—and I'm still doing it. All families deserve a shot at their dreams, and they deserve a country that supports them in that pursuit. That's why this work is worth it. If we come together in grace, we can make a difference.

ONE HUNDRED YEARS AGO, A CURIOUS LITTLE BOY IN AN English village bent down to pick up a piece of metal he saw lying in the dirt. The object, a shell from the First World War, suddenly exploded, mangling the boy's left arm. With the nearest hospital miles away, and no car to take him there, there was no possibility of saving his damaged limb. That's how, in one horrifying instant, Al Rowe was transformed from a carefree boy to a young man with an uncertain future.

This terrible accident would have been traumatic for anyone, but young Al displayed a resilience beyond his years. Undaunted, he forged ahead, learning how to do everything he'd done before, never complaining about the difficulties he must have endured. Not only did he take up soccer, but he began playing golf, too, swinging the club one-handed with surprising strength and precision. And in 1923 when he got past that frightening detention at Ellis Island and entered the United States as a new immigrant, he was determined to create a better life for himself and for the family he hoped one day to have.

Al Rowe was an American patriot through and through. He wanted to give back to the community, so in addition to the hours he spent working on the floor of that New Jersey pencil factory, he ran for a seat on the town council of Wood-Ridge. He rose to become council president, which meant that whenever the mayor was out of town, he would take over for the day. He was also active with the Elks and at charity events, and he never missed any of his son's baseball games. He was immensely proud of his country and proud of the work he did in our town.

My grandfather was a strong man. I loved him dearly, and I knew of only two things he couldn't do: tie his shoes and button his right sleeve. That never bothered him; he would just ask my grandmother, Uncle Jack, or my mother to help him do it. If there's one word that sums up my grandfather, it's resilience. He survived a hideous injury, but he overcame his disability and lived a full, honorable life. He got knocked down, just as we all do. But he never failed to get up, again and again.

NOT LONG AGO, I WAS TALKING WITH A FRIEND WHO WORKED in national security for the Obama administration. He made the comment that resilience has always been one of America's greatest strengths. Whenever we've made mistakes or suffered dreadful losses, we've recovered quickly. It's in our nature to look to the future, and when faced with a critical situation, we have always unified as a nation. Throughout our history, the American people have tended to believe that our country is headed in the right direction, and that has made it easier for us to rebound from setbacks.

But now my friend was troubled. In recent years, he observed, we have seemed to be losing that resilience, and other countries are taking note. These days, our politicians, our parties, and our people are turning on one another with alarming ferocity. Mistrust has become the norm, and disagreements are too often personal. Political ambition has compromised the core functioning of our democracy, resulting in power plays such as the GOP's blocking Merrick Garland from his chance at a seat on the Supreme Court, or changing the filibuster rules in the Senate. Democrats and Republicans have always had different ideas about how to move forward, but now we can't even agree on what's fact and what's fake. We're so focused on opposing each other that I sometimes think we've forgotten the most essential fact: we're all Americans and we're all in this together.

How did this happen? When, and why, did the fabric of our

nation become so frayed? I believe that at least part of the answer can be traced back to the September 11 attacks—or, more precisely, to the months and years that followed 9/11.

In the first days after those horrific attacks, Americans came together, stronger than ever. Volunteers streamed into New York City to help excavate the pile at Ground Zero. People donated clothing, toys, and cash for those displaced by the disaster. Home owners who had never flown an American flag outside their front doors proudly displayed the colors. And although the Twin Towers had fallen, Americans rallied behind the idea of building an even taller skyscraper, the Freedom Tower, where the destroyed buildings had once stood.

If the terrorists had thought they could divide us, they were wrong—at least, that's how it felt in those early days. Now, seventeen years later, the wounds inflicted on that terrifying morning seem to have festered and become something even worse. Rather than welcoming new immigrants with open arms, we've become a nation of travel bans and walls. Rather than championing the freedoms that have long served as the foundation of our country (freedom of religion, of speech, of the press), we've become less tolerant, more authoritarian, and more suspicious of our fellow citizens.

We've become increasingly alienated from one another, and we're alienating the rest of the world, too. In the weeks following 9/11, nearly every nation stood with us in an unprecedented display of global unity. That same year, we properly responded to the attacks with Operation Enduring Freedom in Afghanistan. Eighteen months later, however, our military invaded Iraq, marking the start of an appalling, misguided war. Six trillion dollars and thousands of casualties later, we've succeeded only in descending into a quagmire we are still struggling to get out of. In the process, we have radicalized a new anti-American generation abroad and stoked the fires of xenophobia in our own land. In 2016, this led directly to the election of a president whose isolationist, intolerant, inflammatory words and actions have served only to divide us further.

I find all this extremely troubling, not just as a patriot who loves his country but also as a father of four daughters. My children are growing up in an age of casual cruelty and mean-spiritedness, made all the worse by how fast this sort of poisonous behavior spreads online. It's painful to see my girls try to make sense of a world in which civility has been badly devalued, of a president who regularly tweets insults, engages in bullying and name-calling, proudly displays sexist tendencies, and refers to developing countries as s**tholes.

Are we seeing the beginning of the end of the post–World War II era of American strength and global leadership? Many people seem to think so. When Angela Merkel, the chancellor of Germany, essentially declares that the European Union can no longer depend upon the United States, that's a blow to our standing. When numerous other nations band together in trade agreements and environmental initiatives while we choose to remain on the sidelines, we damage our position in the world order.

Eliot Cohen, a lifelong Republican and the director of the Strategic Studies Program at the Johns Hopkins University School of Advanced International Studies, summed up the problem in a devastating *Atlantic* magazine article, "How Trump Is Ending the American Era."

America's astonishing resilience may rescue it once again, particularly if Trump does not finish his first term. But an equally likely scenario is that Trump will leave key government institutions weakened or corrupted, America's foreign-policy establishment sharply divided, and America's position in the world stunted. An America lacking confidence, coupled with the rise of undemocratic powers, populist movements on the right and left, and failing states, is the kind of world few Americans remember. It would be like the world of the late 1920s or early 1930s: disorderly and unstable, but with much worse to follow.

How can we regain our confidence and restore the resilience that has for so long been our greatest strength? We must start by finding a way to regain the unity and sense of purpose that form the cornerstone of the American experience. And the best way to do that is by electing a leader who stands up for those traits, who unifies us instead of turning us against one another. The president of the United States must lead by example, showing the American people that there's a better way—that we can see both sides, effect compromise, and treat each other with respect. We need a president who can restore America's strength and its position of global leadership.

MANY PEOPLE HAVE ASKED ME WHY I AM RUNNING FOR president. Why me? Why now? As an entrepreneur, CEO, and three-term member of Congress, I don't have a conventional résumé for a politician, much less a candidate for president. But I'm convinced that the skills I've developed over my multifaceted career have prepared me for the office of the presidency. I'm not a lifetime politician, and I'm not a one-dimensional businessman.

What I am is a pragmatic idealist, a person who has spent three decades assessing problems frankly, taking in all points of view, and charting the wisest course of action—for everything from my family and my companies to nonprofit boards, from the Sixth District of Maryland to the Congress of the United States.

I am running for president because the cost of doing nothing is not nothing. The longer we put off fixing the problems currently afflicting our nation, the worse they're going to get. During my time in Congress, I've been struck by how little we actually do. I am confident that, as president, I will take the necessary steps to turn our country around. It's time to look squarely at the facts, assess them honestly, and draw upon the best ideas from both sides of the aisle to formulate creative and effective solutions to our problems.

A good president is steady, stable, honest, and optimistic. He or she creates a sense of greater purpose for the American people and fosters a sense of confidence in where the country is heading, which in turn fuels the resilience we need whenever things go wrong. We can't know what crises will arise in the course of any given presidency, so it's more important than ever to elect someone to the office who is capable of handling whatever challenges we'll face in the future. We need someone who will never for an instant forget that the only interests that matter are those that serve our nation and all its people. Only then can we begin steering ourselves to the better future our citizens deserve.

Instead of spending precious resources fighting to stay afloat, we can become the kind of country in which equality is not just a word we say but a tenet we live by. We can renew our commitment to creating a just and well-educated society and applying our laws to the powerful and the disadvantaged alike. We can redouble our efforts to work toward eliminating poverty and making sure no child in this, the most powerful nation on earth, goes hungry.

By embracing the great forces of economic change, we can build a robust economy that benefits both workers and investors, where capitalism becomes more just and inclusive, and where companies commit to serving a larger social purpose. We can create a world where our entrepreneurs continue to lead the charge and serve as our champions of innovation, building great and enduring businesses that employ millions of people and effect positive societal change.

We can strive toward a world where, through our nation's inspired leadership, we can eliminate the threat of nuclear weapons and help nurture stability and peace in countries riven by conflict and war. We can make further strides in eliminating the diseases that ravage so many people here and abroad, and we can lead the increasingly urgent effort to combat climate change. And we can once again become leaders in the noble effort to spread justice and freedom across the globe.

These are the ideals that have, for centuries, led people such as Albert Rowe to risk everything to come to our shores. These ideals are the beating heart of our great nation, and they are worth fighting for every day of our lives. They can—and with the right leadership, they will—lead the American people into the future with a renewed sense of strength and hope.

ACKNOWLEDGMENTS

This is my first book, and writing it has given me an opportunity to reminisce and reflect on the many people who have played important roles in my life. I'd like to close with my deepest appreciation to them.

I'll start with my family. April, Summer, Brooke, Lily, and Grace, I am a blessed man to have you in my life. My mom, dad, and sister, Diane, you mean the world to me.

I want to thank April's mom, Laurel, and her late dad, Tom, not only for raising an amazing daughter but also for the sacrifice of having her live on the other side of the country.

The star of the book is my grandfather Al Rowe, whose story inspires me now in ways I could never fully appreciate as a boy. But my memories of all four of my grandparents are warm. It is a blessing for kids to be around loving grandparents, as my own children have been.

I want to thank those who so generously provided quotes of support in advance of this book's publication: Steve Case, Stan McChrystal, José Andrés, Katherine Bradley, Joe Kennedy, Sonal Shah, Richard Hanna, Jim Sorenson, and Elijah Cummings. Taking the time to read a book and provide a quote is a heavy lift, and I'm grateful.

As Santa says in my daughters' favorite holiday movie, *The Polar Express*, "there is no greater gift than friendship," and in this category April and I have been truly blessed. We have made dear friends at our kids' schools (St. Patrick's, Potomac, Stone Ridge, Community School); at our church, Little Flower Parish; and in our local communities in Chevy Chase and Columbia. And to my friends back home in New Jersey; in our special places in Idaho and Rehoboth; and in our schools, our boards, and in other communities, including Georgetown and Northwestern—too many people to mention—I thank you all.

April and I also want to extend a special thanks to all those who have gone out of their way to do something specific to make a difference in my campaign or for our family since we started our journey in public service, including: Katherine and David Bradley, Marianne and Keith Powell, Steve and Susie Canton, Raul and Jean-Marie Fernandez, Kay Kendall and Jack Davies, Anna and Paul Collins, Amy and Alan Meltzer, Beth and Ron Dozoretz, Steve and Jean Case, Steve and Sue Mandel, Jason and Courtney Fish, George and Lori Harrop, Robert and Anna Trone, Stephanie and Dan Lennon, Matt Wagner, Andrew Feldstein, Chris and Karen Donatelli, Donn Davis, Anne and Ray Ritchey, Connie and Eric Lindenauer, Mary and Bobby Haft, Steve Fishman, Arnie Whitman, Ben Jacobs, Willy and Sheila Walker, Carol and Gene Ludwig, Joe Jolson, Carter Mack, Peter Barrett, Larry Culp, Matt

Botein, Sam Spiritos, Karen and Ethan Leder, Lisa and Steven Tananbaum, Brendan Carroll, Bill Duhamel, Jim and Tracy Racheff, Myrna Whitworth, Hillary Kapner, Jason Moment, Robin Summerfield, Nancy Eristoff, Mona Hanaford, Deb Graham, Rocky Fried, Steve and Anne Arcano, Nancy and Mark Duber, Ned Johnson, Lynn and Greg O'Brien, Jimmy Reyes, Jack DeGoia, Jim Johnson, Howard and Nick Fineman, Amy Nathan, Rick Schifter, Ron Halber, Jane and Esko Korhonen, Steve Whelen, Mike and Lynn Novelli, Mimi Hassanein, Steve and Ashley Quamme, Paul and Chan Tagliabue, Chris Jones, Rob Rubin, Stu Bloch, Jeff Neuchterlein, David and Marijke Dupree, Neil and Marci Cohen, Tom Ruhf, Alexander Arata, Morty Schapiro, Josh Gillon, Martha and Walter Spak, Nick and Alyssa Lovegrove, Larry Brown, Ralph Masino, Marjorie Brennan, John Kowalik, Mark and Sally Ein, Roger and Vicki Sant, Barbara O'Keefe, Andy Cornblatt, Terry McAuliffe, Patty Durkin Trinker, Paul Wilner, Allison and Kai Reynolds, John Lane, Lenora and John Lynham, Jack and Val Rowe, Kimm and Al Uzelli, Jay and John Rogovin, Lee Satterfield and Patrick Steel, Chip Cook, Mellissa and Greg Gregorian, Carlos Montenegro, Rob Stewart, Mae and Andy Grennan, Patrick Baugh and Michael DeSantis, and Allison and John Shulman.

"If you want to go fast, go alone. If you want to go far, go together" is a proverb that pretty well sums up my career.

I'd like to thank everyone who's worked or volunteered on my political campaigns and those who have worked in my office on Capitol Hill, including Xan Fishman, Will McDonald, Lisa Bianco, Justin Schall, John Monsif, Liz Jaff, Lauren Santabar, Kevin Mack, Sonny Holding, and Ben Turner. Xan and Will deserve particular thanks for their help on this book and their true loyalty across the years.

I also want to thank my group of friends who have over the years offered tremendous policy and political advice, including: Jeff Zients, Ron Klain, Tom Nides, Margie Sullivan, Peter Scher, Bill Knapp, Terry Lierman, Brian Graham, Fred Yang, Mickey Kantor, Jimmy Siegel, Tom Donilon, Dan Glickman, Harrison Hickman, and John Davis. Thanks also to all those who endorsed me when I first ran, including President Bill Clinton, Doug Duncan, Donna Edwards, Peter Franchot, Dee Dee Myers, and the various editorial boards who placed their trust in me. I hope I have earned it.

In business, I've been fortunate to work with great people and forge terrific friendships. I'm grateful to my cofounders at CapitalSource, HealthCare Financial Partners, and Alliance Partners for being such great partners: Jason Fish, Ethan Leder, Ed Nordberg, and Lee Sachs. Over the years, I've had many investors and lenders who backed my various ventures, most notably Tom Steyer, Tim Hurd, Eric Eubank, Tully Friedman, Jim Sigman, and Jeff Perlowitz. I've been lucky enough to work with great senior teams, board members, key advisers, and personal assistants who have also become good friends, including Steve Museles, Dean Graham, Jim Pieczynski, Don Cole, Natasha Luddington, Bryan Corsini, Carey Snyder, Anne Balcer, Mike Szwajkowski, Vicki Landry, David Martin, Joe Kenary, Erik Lindenauer, Kim Pate, Howard Widra, Chris Hague, Chris Kelly, Jeff Galle, Laird Boulden, Rich Lerner, John Simmons, Dennis Oakes, Craig Stine, Ernesto Cruz, Tom Fink, Amy Heller, Tad Lowrey, Steve Curwin, Jeff Lipson, Steve Silver, Hilde Alter, Lori Bettinger, Matt Botein, Kori Ogrosky, Andy Fremder, Larry Nussdorf, Bill Byrnes, Bill Hosler, Chris Woods, John Protzman, Sara Grootwassink, Geoff Brooke, Jim Showen, David Hermer,

Kenny Elias, Keith Rueben, Jeff Lipson, and the late John Dealy. Thank you to all my partners, team members, investors, advisers, and clients for helping to make our journey through the business world successful and rewarding.

I am grateful to law enforcement and first responders for keeping us safe.

April and I have been guided in our lives by inspiring faith leaders, including Cardinals Wuerl and McCarrick, Monsignor Peter Vaghi of Little Flower Parish, and Father John Enzler. Thank you for giving us something more than just hope; we have felt the power of your prayers as we have taken this journey of public service.

In the U.S. Congress, it has been a true honor to serve under the extraordinary Democratic leadership team of Nancy Pelosi, Steny Hoyer, and Jim Clyburn and with other icons of American political life and social justice. I'm grateful to the Maryland delegation for having been so welcoming and to the many members on both sides of the aisle with whom I worked on legislation and now call friends. Before announcing my run for president, I received helpful advice from several colleagues, including Don Beyer, Derek Kilmer, Cheri Bustos, Jamie Raskin, Ro Khanna, Denny Heck, John Larson, Scott Peters, Dan Kildee, John Carney, and Juan Vargas; I'm grateful to you all. Finally, my thanks to my fellow representatives from the freshman class of the 113th Congress, the greatest class yet! My thanks also to all the dedicated public servants I worked so closely with in the Obama administration and to President Obama for his leadership.

I'd also like to thank the people who helped me create and craft this book. To Don Weisberg, thank you for pushing me to write it and for taking such good care of me; April and I are fortunate to have you and Erin as friends. I would not have been able to pull this together without the talents and sense of humor of my new friend, collaborator Lisa Dickey, as well as John Sterling and Paul Golob (and Makaiah, Ahmed, and Tony for helping to pick out the cover!). Several people read all or parts of the book before it was released, including Ned Mandel, Eric London, Mark Steitz, Dave Trott, Sue Mandel, and Seth Klarman—thank you for spending the time on it.

I want to thank our military veterans and the men and women who serve our country today, putting themselves in the position to make the ultimate sacrifice for our freedom.

I want to thank my wonderful constituents in Maryland's Sixth District. Thank you for giving me the opportunity to serve you. It has been an honor and a privilege.

Finally, I thank God, always and for everything.

INDEX

Aetna, 49
Affordable Care Act "Obamacare" (ACA, 2017), 21–22, 39–43, 83, 134
Afghanistan, 189, 203
African Americans, 143
African immigrants, 67
AI Caucus, 176, 178
Alabama, 130
Alzheimer's, 143
Amazon, 33, 102
American dream, 50–51, 77, 148
American Home Therapies, 91–92
American ideals, 6, 17, 206–7
AmeriCorps, 59
Appalachian Mountains, 51
Apple, 33–34
apprenticeships, 58–60, 62, 100, 174
Arlington National Cemetery, 50, 190
artificial intelligence (AI), 4, 143, 176–79, 184
arts education, 181
Asia, 184, 187
Assad, Bashar al-, 189

asthma, 115–18
Atlantic, 204–5
Authorization for Use of Military Force (AUMF, 2001), 144, 190–91
autism, 143
automation, 4, 80, 179

Baier, Bret, 132
Bank Enterprise Award, 111
Bank of England, 81
bankruptcy, 124
banks, 10, 108–9, 120
Bartlett, Roscoe, 146–47, 151
Bayh, Birch, 113
Berkshire Hathaway, 86
Beth Israel Hospital (Boston), 48
Bezos, Jeff, 37
bilingual students, 54
biotechnology, 101
bipartisanship
    AI and, 177
    annual Christmas party and, 136–38
    deficit and, 170–73

bipartisanship (*cont'd*)
  EITC and, 79–80
  George Washington and, 28–29
  health care and, 41–43, 135
  immigration and, 172–73
  importance of, 5, 8–9, 28–29, 38–39,
    75, 100, 136–44, 194–95
  infrastructure and, 23–26, 34–38
  Investing in Opportunity Act and,
    100–103
  Medicaid and, 135
  Patent and Trademark Law Amend-
    ments Act and, 113–14
  pay-for-success programs and, 119
  pre-K and, 55–57
  primary system and, 152
  prioritizing, as president, 43–46,
    140–44
  Reagan and, 78–79, 161–62
  Social Security and, 8, 159–63
  taxes and, 78–79
  veterans and, 191
  vocational training and, 58–59
BlackBerry, 111
block grants, 56
Boston, 49, 101
Bowles, Erskine, 171–72
Boys and Girls Club, 107
Bradley, Carter, 165
Bradley, David, 165–67
Bradley, Katherine, 164–65
British Parliament, 17
broadband Internet, 30, 101–2, 143
Bryce Mountain, Virginia, 197
Budget Control Act (2011), 172
Buffett, Warren, 86
Buffett rule, 173
Buhl, Idaho, 74
Bush, George W., 172, 191
business and entrepreneurship. *See also* jobs
  career in, 6, 13–15, 25–26, 47, 50,
    70–73, 77, 89–94, 98, 106, 108–12,
    119–23, 146, 164
  government and, 99, 112–13, 124–25,
    141
  health insurance and, 83
  immigration and, 173
  patents and, 113–14

  pay-for-success programs and, 116–19
  politics vs., 5, 97, 148–49
  principles of successful, 13–14, 94–99,
    123–24, 207
  rare diseases program and, 114
  vocational training and, 58–59

cable television, 46
California, 101, 152
campaign finance, 146
cancer, 91, 143
capital gains taxes, 102–3, 125
capitalism, 86–87, 207
capital markets, 120–21, 129
CapitalSource, 14–15, 108–12, 119–23,
  128–30, 146
capitation model, 91
carbon emissions, 81–82, 143, 172
caregivers, 182
Carney, Mark, 81
carried interest loophole, 174
Catholic Charities, 107
Catholic Church, 136
census, 147
Center for Urban Families (Baltimore), 107
Centers for Disease Control and
  Prevention, 115
charitable donations, 77–78
charter schools, 56
checks and balances, 16
chemical weapons, 189
Chicago Public Schools, 52–54
child care, 182
children
  hunger and, 144
  investing in, 174
  media literacy and, 75
  raising, 198–200
Children's National Medical Center, 107
China, 167, 187, 192
church-based programs, 56
Churchill, Winston, 127
CIT Corporation, 15, 122
civics literacy, 60
Civilian Conservation Corps (CCC), 63
civility, 15, 21–22, 75, 204–5
Civil Rights Act (1964), 158
Claypoole's American Daily Advertiser, 26

climate change, 79, 80–82, 143, 167–68, 207
Clinton, Bill, 151
Clinton, Hillary, Fellowship, 107
coal industry, 82
Cohen, Eliot, 204–5
Cole, Tom, 159, 163
collateralized debt obligations (CDOs), 120–21
colleges and universities, 48–54, 61–62, 68, 113. *See also* community colleges; student debt; vocational training
Columbia-Presbyterian Medical Center, 69
Columbia University, 49–50, 68–69
Common Sense Media, 75, 107
Communications Act (1934), 75
communities
    of color, 66–67, 143
    globalization and, 20, 101–2, 168, 183–84
    investment in distressed, 101–2
community colleges, 58, 168, 174, 180
Community Foundation of the National Capital Region, 106
Community School (Idaho), 107
community service, 59–60, 142
competitiveness, 141, 175
compromise, 4–5, 55–56, 135, 205
Congressional Budget Office, 83
Congressional Club, 138
construction, 6, 10–12, 31, 70
consumer lending, 109
Cook, Tim, 34
corporate taxes, 32–35, 173
    foreign cash and, 24, 32–38, 79, 154–55
crash of 1929, 64
criminal justice reform, 118, 143
Cumberland, Maryland, 51
Cuomo, Mario, 145
cyber-bullying, 75, 143

Dalio, Ray, 65
DC General Hospital (Washington, DC), 90–91
Dealy, John, 76
Deep Blue, 176

Defense Department, 190
DeGioia, Jack, 157
Delaney, Brooke (daughter), 106, 148, 150, 200
Delaney, Diane (sister), 10, 13
Delaney, Elaine Rowe (mother), 3, 10, 12–14, 25, 48, 68, 150
Delaney, Grace (daughter), 148, 150, 199, 200
Delaney, Jack (father), 3, 9–13, 25, 48–49, 69
Delaney, Lily (daughter), 106, 148, 150, 199, 200
Delaney, Summer (daughter), 92, 106–7, 148, 150, 165, 196–98, 199–200
Delaney Family Fund, 106–7
democracy, 15–16, 26–27, 60, 153
Democratic National Committee (DNC), 145
Democratic National Convention (1936), 63–65
Democratic Party, 5, 45, 127–28, 130, 150–51
    deficits and, 103–5
    EITC and, 80
    gerrymandering and, 147, 151, 153
    health care and, 42–43, 133–35
    infrastructure and, 23–24, 36, 38
    Investing in Opportunity Act and, 103
    partisanship and, 98, 130–31, 139, 202
    pre-K and, 55–56
    Reagan tax cuts and, 78–79
    Social Security and, 160–63
    trade and, 184
    values and ideals of, 29, 97–98
Democratic Party Caucus, 45, 127–28, 130, 145–46
Depression, 63
digital literacy, 75
diplomacy, 174, 186, 188
discrimination, 43, 158
Dodd-Frank Wall Street Reform and Consumer Protection Act (2010), 123
Doherty, Carroll, 140
Dole, Bob, 113
dot-com boom, 108
Douglass, Frederick, 7

Dreamers, 172
drinking age, minimum, 61–61
Duncan, Doug, 147–48

Earned Income Tax Credit (EITC),
    79–80, 174, 181–82
Eccles, David, 192
economic growth, 4, 20, 30, 63–64, 82,
    101–2, 104–5, 170, 207
economic mobility, 51, 80, 167
Economic Opportunity Act (1964),
    158
Economist, 114
education, 48–59, 66, 68, 79, 98,
    107, 142, 158, 168, 178, 193,
    206. *See also* colleges and
    universities; community colleges;
    pre-kindergarten; skills gap; voca-
    tional training
Einstein, Albert, 89
Election Day, as federal holiday, 152
elections
    of 1932, 64
    of 2012, 30, 148–51
    of 2016, 4, 60, 152, 182, 187–88,
        204
    of 2017, 130
    of 2020, 175
    proposed reforms for, 152
electricians, 10–12, 25–26, 48–50, 69
Elementary and Secondary Education Act
    (ESEA, 1965)
Elks Club, 201
Ellis Island, 2–3, 47–48, 201
employee benefits, 84–85, 87, 110–11,
    180
energy, 101, 174
Enron, 129
environmental policy, 87, 140, 186
estate tax, 77–78, 174
European Union, 204
exports, 184–85
ExxonMobil, 81

Facebook Live, 18, 178
Fairleigh Dickinson University, 25–26
family leave, paid, 110, 180
Farallon Capital Management, 93, 109

federal budget, 22, 57, 190. *See also* gov-
    ernment; taxes
    deficits and, 31, 103–5, 132
    mandatory spending programs,
        168–69, 171, 175
    spending and revenue plan and,
        169–73
Federal Communications Commission
    (FCC), 63
Federal Deposit Insurance Corporation
    (FDIC), 63
Federal Reserve, 160
FICA tax, 168, 174
financial crisis of 2008, 14–15, 119–23,
    146
financial literacy, 60
financial services companies, 14–15, 87,
    92–93, 109–11
First Union, 109
Fish, Jason, 93, 109, 111, 128
Flint, Michigan, 30
Food and Drug Administration (FDA),
    114
Food Stamp Program, 158
foreign policy, 186–91
Fortune "World's 50 Greatest Leaders,"
    37
fossil fuels, 82
401(k) plans, 110
France, 57–58
Francis, Pope, 37
Franconia, RMS (ship), 2
Franklin, Benjamin, 106
Freedom Tower, 203
Fremont Capital, 121
Fresno, California, 116–17
Friends of St. Patrick's, 166
future, preparing for, 4, 6, 167–69,
    184–85, 194–95
FUTURE of AI Act (proposed), 177

Gaithersburg, Maryland, 7–9, 100
Garagiola, Rob, 147–48, 150–51
Garland, Merrick, 202
gas tax, 132–33, 172
Gates Foundation, 117
gazelles (fast-growing midsize
    companies), 110

Georgetown University, 136
    Center on Education and the Work-
        force, 180
    Institute for Women, Peace, and
        Security, 107
    Law Center, 69, 72–74, 76, 107,
        157
George Washington Bridge, 48
George Washington University, 165
Germany, 32–33, 204
gerontology, 48
gerrymandering, 87–88, 142, 147,
    151–54
Giants Stadium (New Jersey), 10
Gingrich, Newt, 155
girls, issues concerning, 107–8
global alliances, 4, 168, 188
globalization, 19–21, 31, 80–81, 100–
    101, 182–83. *See also* international
    tax system
global leadership, 187–89, 192–93,
    204–5, 207
Google, 33, 176
Google for Jobs, 180
Google X, 178
government. *See also* federal budget
    branches of, 16
    incentives and, 77–78
    infrastructure and, 101–2
    innovation and, 113, 124–26
    job of legislating and, 154–55
    private sector and, 114–18
    responsibility to people and, 99–100
    restoring trust in, 15–22
    universal pre-K and, 55
    weakening of, 204–5
GovTrack.us, 8
Grameen Bank, 96–97
"greater fool" theory, 108
Greater Southeast Hospital (Washington,
    DC), 90–91
Greenspan, Alan, 160
"grinding out the details," 25–26
gun safety, 21, 142

Harris, Kamala, 152
Harvard University, 48, 90
Hasbrouck Heights, New Jersey, 10

Head Start, 56, 158
health care, 39, 40–43, 48–49, 84,
    142–44, 168, 175, 207. *See also*
    Affordable Care Act; Medicaid;
    Medicare
    decoupling from employment, 82–85,
        124, 180
    exchanges and, 40–41
    fixes for, 99, 131, 133–34
    incentives and, 82–86
    jobs in, 181
    private sector and, 115–16
    veterans and, 144
HealthCare Financial Partners (*for-
    merly* HealthPartners Financial
    Corporation), 47, 92–94, 98, 106,
    109, 112, 164
health insurance, 41–42, 82–85, 91–92,
    110
HealthPartners Financial Corporation.
    See HealthCare Financial Partners
Heller Financial, 94
Highway Trust Fund, 35, 132
Hispanic population, 54
HIV/AIDS, 91
Holland Tunnel, 48
home health care companies, 89–91
home infusion companies, 91
Homeland Security Department, 169
homelessness, 144
home mortgages, 104
home ownership, 3, 10, 12–13, 101
hospitals, 40, 116–17
    uncompensated care and, 84
hot money investors, 120–21
"How Trump Is Ending the American
    Era" (Cohen), 204–5
Hoyer, Steny, 137
Hurd, Tim, 109

IBM, 176
Idaho, 149
Idaho Potato Farmers Association, 74
Ignatius of Loyola, St., 136
immigration, 1–3, 47–48, 50, 140,
    172–73, 201
immigration reform bill (2013), 172–73
impact investors, 54, 55, 117–18

incentives, 68
    civic life and, 77–78
    climate change and, 80–82
    distressed communities and, 102, 168
    EITC and, 79–80
    health care and, 83–86
    taxes and, 79
    workers and, 87, 181
income inequality, 4, 20, 63–67, 86
independent contractors, 180
Independents, 152–53
inflation, 132, 171
information technology, 101
infrastructure, 30–32, 60, 62, 79, 99,
        101–2, 132–33, 141, 167, 174–75,
        183, 185
infrastructure bank, 35
infrastructure bill (proposed bipartisan),
        24–26, 29–30, 34–38, 100, 102,
        146, 154–55, 168
innovation, 99, 113–17
insecurity, 167–68
insurance companies, 120
intellectual property, 33, 35
interest rates, 104
International Brotherhood of Electrical
        Workers (IBEW), 10
    Local 164, 48–50, 93
International Center for Research on
        Women, 107
international tax system, 32, 35, 154–55
Internet start-ups, 108
Investing in Opportunity Act (2017),
        100–103
Iraq, 203
Irish Americans, 9–10
isolationism, 4, 167–68, 188, 204
Israel, 188

Japan, 188
Jersey (island), 33, 35
Jersey City, New Jersey, 9–10, 48, 49, 93
Job Corps, 158
jobs, 4, 6, 14, 30, 101, 110, 112, 167, 207
    benefits and, 82–85, 87, 110–11, 180
    community college and, 58
    future of work and, 180–82
    globalization and, 183–86

infrastructure and, 30–31, 101
    outsourcing, 101, 183
    technology and, 179–80
    TPP and, 184–85
    vocational training and, 58–60
Johns Hopkins University, 178, 204
Johnson, Lyndon Baines, 157–58
Joint Select Committee on Deficit Reduc-
        tion (Supercommittee), 172
Joint Special Operations Command, 189
Jones, Doug, 130
Joseph Dixon Crucible Company, 3
JPMorgan, 123
JUST Capital, 87

Kaiser Permanente, 91
Kasich, John, 37
Kasparov, Garry, 176
Keller, Helen, 23
Kennedy, John F., 6, 191–95

labor unions, 12, 48–50, 58, 60, 183
Lautenberg, Frank, 62
leadership, 4–6, 187–89, 192–93, 204–7
Leddel Health, 90
Leder, Ethan, 89–92, 94, 98
Lehman Brothers, 122
Lightner, Candace, 61
Lightner, Cari, 61
Lincoln Tunnel, 48
low- and middle-income families, 82
low-income students, 52–54
Lowry, Marianne, 91
LSAT, 69

Madison Dearborn Company, 109
manufacturing, 31, 101, 185
market-based solutions, 96–97
marketization of uncompensated work, 182
Maryland
    Cumberland, 51
    Gaithersburg, 7–9, 100
    Sixth District, 8, 146–47, 151, 206
Maryland Democratic primary of 2012,
        150–51
Maryland State Senate, 147
Mason City, Iowa, 130–31
McAdams, Ben, 54–55

McChrystal, Stanley, 59, 189
McClain-Delaney, April (wife), 73–76, 92, 107, 136–39, 148–50, 157, 165, 196, 198–99
McConnell, Mitch, 154
McKinsey & Company, 179
Meadowlands, 48, 70
Medicaid, 85, 168
    asthma and, 115–17
    expansion and reform of, 39–40, 83–84, 86, 133–35
    home health care and, 90
Medicare, 8, 40, 168
    buy-ins for over-55, 41–42, 131
    cost of, 85, 175
    drug prices and, 42
    home health care and, 90
    public option and, 83
mental health care, 86, 142
Merkel, Angela, 37, 204
Messer, Jennifer, 138
Messer, Luke, 138
Metcalfe, Richard, 92–93
micro-lending, 95–96, 98
middle class, global, 20, 183, 185–86
military readiness, 144, 187–91
military service, 59–61
military spending, 169, 174
minority groups, 158
moderate voters, 130
monetary policy, 31
Montessori, 56
Montgomery County, Maryland, 75, 147
Moore, Roy, 130
Mothers Against Drunk Driving (MADD), 61
Mount Sinai–New York University Medical Center and Health System, 48
Munger, Charlie, 68, 86
Musk, Elon, 177

NASDAQ, 93
National Commission on Fiscal Responsibility and Reform (Simpson-Bowles Commission), 171–72
National Commission on Social Security Reform (Greenspan Commission), 8, 160–62

national debt, 31, 105, 169–71
National Endowment for the Arts, 158
National Endowment for the Humanities, 158
National Minimum Drinking Age Act (1984), 61–62
national security, 140, 144, 168, 187, 188. See also military readiness
national service, 59–63, 100, 141, 174
National Symphony Orchestra, 107
Neglected Tropical Disease Priority Review Voucher Program, 114
New Deal, 63
New Jersey, 9–10, 70
New York City, 101, 203
New York Stock Exchange (NYSE), 47, 50, 93, 111, 121
New York Times, 1, 33
Nobel Peace Prize, 96
no-fly list, 22
Nolan, Rich, 156
nonprofits, 113–17
Nordberg, Ed, 92, 94, 98
Norquist, Grover, 131, 133
North Atlantic Treaty Organization (NATO), 188
North Korea, 187
Northwestern University, 52–54, 107
    Academy for Chicago Public Schools, 53–54
nuclear weapons, 144, 188, 207

Obama, Barack, 24, 111, 146, 154, 171, 173, 189, 202
Obamacare. See Affordable Care Act
oil companies, 81
One Belt, One Road policy, 167
O'Neill, Thomas "Tip," 8, 160–63
Open Our Democracy Act (proposed), 152–54
Operation Enduring Freedom, 203
opioid epidemic, 142, 167
opportunity, 6, 50–51, 67, 79
opportunity zones, 102
"original path to yes" principle, 94
"Our Biggest Economic, Social, and Political Issue" (Dalio), 65–66

parenting, 198–200
Paris Climate Accords, 81
partisanship, 3–6, 13–17, 21, 46, 100,
    139–40, 154–55, 202. *See also* bipar-
    tisanship
  ACA and, 39–40
  George Washington on, 26–29
  globalization and, 184
  as impediment to governing,
    158–60
  incentives and, 87–88
  infrastructure and, 24–26, 36
Patent and Trademark Law Amendments
    Act (Bayh-Dole, 1980), 113–14
pay cuts, 183
Pay-for-Success programs, 55, 115,
    117–18, 180
payroll tax, 168
Peace Corps, 59
Pelosi, Nancy, 38
pension funds, 120
Pew Research Center, 16, 139–40
pharmaceutical companies, 42, 84, 114.
    See also prescription drugs
philanthropy, 6, 54, 57, 106–8, 116–18,
    142, 164
Pitofsky, Alex, 69
Potomac School, 107
poverty, 51, 144, 206–7
  EITC and, 79–80
  globalization and, 20, 183, 186
  infrastructure and, 30
  mental health and, 86
  micro-loans and, 96
  Social Security and, 8, 162
pragmatism, 5, 100, 206
pre-kindergarten (pre-K), 54–57, 115,
    168, 174
prescription drugs, 143, 175. *See also*
    pharmaceutical companies
president's weekly radio address, 18
primary elections, 152–53
privacy, 75, 143
private sector, 101–2, 113–15
progressive ideals, 9, 96–98, 118
public education, 55–58, 75, 141. *See also*
    education; pre-kindergarten
public health clinics, 86

public option, 83–84, 175
public-private partnerships, 58–59, 100,
    113–14
Public Works Administration (PWA),
    63

Question Time, 17

racial issues, 140, 143
Rare Pediatric Disease Priority Review
    Voucher Program, 114–15
Reagan, Ronald, 8, 16, 61, 78, 160–63
real estate development, 70–73, 77
recidivism programs, 118
redistricting, independent commissions
    for, 153
regulations, 125–26, 141
Reiger, Frank, 70
Republican Party, 5, 21, 139–40,
    146–47, 173
  addressing, as president, 45
  Affordable Care Act and, 39
  deficits and, 103–5
  Democratic retreat and, 127–28, 130
  gerrymandering and, 147
  health care and, 42–43
  infrastructure and, 23–25, 31–32,
    36–38
  Investing in Opportunity Act and,
    103
  Medicaid and, 133–35
  partisanship and, 98, 202
  presidential primaries of 2011 and, 132
  Social Security and, 160–63
  taxes and, 32, 37, 77–80, 98, 103,
    131–33, 169–70, 175
  universal pre-K and, 55–56
research and development investment, 79,
    113, 124–25, 143, 174
resilience, 201–7
resources, investing, 171, 174–75
retirement, 66, 124, 180–81
Revolutionary War, 16
risk taking, 83, 113, 124
Romney, Mitt, 40–41
Roosevelt, Eleanor, 164
Roosevelt, Franklin Delano, 47, 63–65,
    159

Rowe, Albert "Al" (grandfather), 2–3, 6, 10, 47–48, 200–202, 207
Rowe, Emily (great-grandmother), 2
Rowe, John "Jack" (uncle), 3, 48–49, 68, 90, 201
Rowe, Percival (great-uncle), 2
Rowe, William (great-grandfather), 2
Running at Criticism tour, 129–30
rural communities, 30, 101–2, 143
Russo, Larry, 70

safety net, 174, 181
Salt Lake County, 54
Sanchez, Loretta, 152
Sanders, Bernie, 182
Sarbanes, Paul, 146
Saria, Suchi, 178
savings rates, 66
Schapiro, Morton, 53
Schuman, Ilyse, 74
Schumer, Chuck, 38
science, technology, engineering, and math (STEM), 143, 175, 181, 192–94
Securities and Exchange Commission (SEC), 63
securitization, 120–21
September 11, 2001, attacks (9/11), 190, 203
sequester, 172, 174
service industries, 101
sexual harassment, 143
Shaw Pittman firm, 76–77
short sellers, 128–30
Sigman, Jim, 109
Simpson, Alan, 171–72
single-payer plans, 84–86, 131
skills gap, 59, 62–63, 79, 100, 141, 167, 174–75, 180, 193
small- to middle-market companies, 109–12
smartphones, 178
social impact bonds, 115, 117
social media, 86, 199
Social Security, 8–9, 100, 159–63, 168, 175
South Korea, 188
Soviet Union, 191–92, 194

space exploration, 191–94
SpaceX, 177
special-needs education, 55
Springsteen, Bruce, 51
Sputnik 1 (satellite), 191
Standard and Poor's, 81
Starbucks, 33, 35
state and local governments, 16, 35, 62, 119
    Medicaid and, 134–35
State of the Union address, 19–21
Statue of Liberty, 47
Steyer, Jim, 75
Steyer, Tom, 93, 109
St. Luke's Hospital, 68
Stone, James, 59
St. Patrick's Episcopal Day School, 107, 164–67
student debt, 62, 99, 104, 124, 167
student grants, 58–59
summer jobs, 69–70, 73
Switzerland, 62
Syria, 189

tariffs, 182
Tax Cuts and Jobs Act (2017), 32, 37, 77, 79, 103, 142, 169–70, 173
taxes, 22. *See also* capital gains taxes; estate tax; *other specific types; and specific bills*
    carbon pricing and, 82
    charitable giving and, 77–78
    corporate foreign cash and, 24, 32–38, 79, 154–55
    deductions and, 173
    deficits and, 31–32
    EITC and, 79–80
    employer-provided health insurance and, 84–85
    incentives and, 103
    payroll, 168–69
    proposed reforms, 171–74
    Republican Party and, 32, 37, 77–80, 98, 103, 131–33, 169–70, 172, 175
    spending priorities and, 169
    tax shelters and, 78
    universal pre-K and, 56–57

Taxpayer Protection Pledge, 131–33
Tax Reform Act (1986), 78
Teach For America, 59
Tea Party Caucus, 146
tech addiction, 75, 143
technological innovation, 4, 19–21, 75, 108, 141, 175–81, 183–84, 192–93
telecommunications, 143
Teller, Edward, 193
terrorism, 20–21, 190–91, 203–4
Tesla, 177
"think different" principle, 94–96
Third Offset Strategy, 190
Thrun, Sebastian, 178
town halls, 7, 45–46
trade, 168, 182–88
Trans-Pacific Partnership (TPP), 184–87
transparency, 14–15, 18, 87
trickle-down economics, 31–32, 80, 170
trickle-up economics, 80
Troubled Asset Relief Program (TARP), 123
Trump, Donald, 16–18, 182, 204–5
    allies and, 188
    debt ceiling and, 38
    opposition to, 7, 9, 93
    Paris climate accord and, 81
    trade and, 186–87
truth telling, 14–15, 17–21
Tucci, Dominic, 70–73, 166
Twitter, 18, 46

unemployment, 51, 59, 101. See also jobs
U.S. Congress
    AI Caucus in, 176
    bipartisan infrastructure legislation and, 23–24, 29–39
    bipartisanship and, 194–95
    budget and, 169, 190
    campaigning vs. governing and, 155–59, 206
    corporate taxes and, 34
    daily breakfast with, as president, 44–45
    getting buy-in from, 99
    Highway Trust Fund and, 132–33

immigration and, 172–73
Simpson-Bowles and, 171–72
Social Security and, 163
space program and, 193
top-two primaries and, 152
TPP and, 184
TV debates with, as president, 17–18
U.S. House of Representatives, 6, 8, 23–24, 29–38, 137, 152, 172–73, 176, 205–6
    campaign of 2012 for, 30, 112, 135–36, 146–52
    freshman term in, 23–24, 26, 35–36, 137–38, 145
U.S. Senate, 24, 130, 152, 172, 202
U.S. Supreme Court, 202
Utah, 115

Verveer, Melanne, 107
veterans, 144, 169, 191
Veterans Affairs Department, 169
Virginia, 149
visa program, 172
Vision to Learn, 107
VISTA program, 158
vocational training, 57–62, 180
Voting Rights Act (1965), 158
voting rights and electoral reform, 152–53

wages, 84, 101
    minimum, 181
wage support program, 181–82
Walmart, 42
Warner, Mark, 149
Washington, DC, zoning board, 166
Washington, George, 26–28
Washington Post, 89, 151
Washington State, 152
wealth concentration, 79. See also income inequality
wealthy, surtax on, 174
Wintergreen, Virginia, 196
women's issues, 75, 107
Wood-Ridge, New Jersey, 48–49, 71–73, 136
Wood-Ridge National Bank, 10
Wood-Ridge town council, 201
Wood-Ridge Zoning Board, 72, 166

work, uncompensated, 182
work ethic, 10–13, 25. *See also* jobs
working class, 6, 70, 82, 148
World War I, 201
"wrong pockets" problem, 116, 119

Young Presidents' Organization, 149
YouTube, 18
Yunus, Muhammad, 95–96, 98

Zients, Jeff, 184

ABOUT THE AUTHOR

JOHN K. DELANEY, the United States representative for Maryland's Sixth Congressional District, was one of America's most innovative and successful entrepreneurs before he entered politics. The cofounder and CEO of two companies, HealthCare Financial and CapitalSource, which were ultimately sold for billions of dollars, he is an active philanthropist. A Democrat who is now in his third term in Congress, he was recently named by *Fortune* magazine as one of the World's 50 Greatest Leaders. Delaney received his undergraduate degree from Columbia University and his J.D. from Georgetown Law. He and his wife, April, have four daughters and live in Montgomery County, Maryland.